Adopted by GOD

Adopted by GOD

From Wayward Sinners to Cherished Children

ROBERT A. PETERSON

P U B L I S H I N G

P.O. BOX 817 • PHILLIPSBURG • NEW JERSEY 08865-0817

Page design by Lakeside Design Plus
Typesetting by Michelle Feaster

Printed in the United States of America

Library of Congress Cataloging-in-Publication Data

Peterson, Robert A., 1948-
    Adopted by God : from wayward sinners to cherished children / Robert A. Peterson.
        p. cm.
    Includes bibliographical references and index.
    ISBN 0-87552-465-6
    1. Adoption (Theology) 2. Adoption (Theology)—Biblical teaching. I. Title.
BT165 .P48 2001
234—dc21

                             2001036896

To the person
who most brilliantly radiates
the Father's love,
Mary Pat

Contents

Foreword

*I*n 1973, James I. Packer wrote his classic study, *Knowing God*. One of the best-known chapters in that book is the one on adoption. In addition to presenting the doctrine itself, Dr. Packer called attention to the fact that both the doctrine of adoption and the implications of that doctrine have been largely overlooked in Christian history. He urged that it be given more attention, and I am pleased that a number of able scholars, teachers, and pastors have taken up his challenge, including Robert Peterson, the author of this volume.

Much as Dr. Packer wanted us to know God, Dr. Peterson wants us to know God as our heavenly Father. We are taken to the Scriptures, both Old and New Testaments, to discover the important relationship between God as our Father and us as his adopted children. It will quickly become apparent to the reader that Dr. Peterson is not satisfied just to inform us about adoption—he wants us to enter personally into the privileges and responsibilities of this extraordinary gift of God. That is a much more biblical use of the word *knowing* than simply the accumulation of valuable information.

In my reading of this book, there were three things that stood out:

1. *It is biblical.* It is clear that Robert Peterson has done his "homework" theologically. Had he chosen to do so, he could have explained adoption from the perspective of systematic theology (which he teaches at Covenant Theological Seminary). But we are constantly challenged instead to reflect on various biblical passages that open up aspects of the theme of sonship. The book has the feel of a theology professor standing before his class—but the class is a group of young people and adults in a church. This is, in fact, how this book originated. Robert has told me that he was struck by the significance of adoption as he taught it in a Sunday school class. In such a setting, he needed to demonstrate the biblical nature of what he was teaching, and that is what he does throughout the book.

2. *It is Trinitarian.* I appreciated the careful presentation of the roles that the persons of the Trinity play in our adoption and sonship. (These two concepts are similar, but not identical. Adoption makes it possible to enter into the relationship of knowing God as sons and daughters—which is our sonship. Many are suggesting that the most appropriate translation for "adoption" in Romans 8:15 and Galatians 4:5 is "adoption unto sonship.") In particular, the author makes sure that we appropriate the work of the Holy Spirit in applying the work ordained by the Father and accomplished by the Son.

There are not only chapters devoted to the distinctive contribution of each member of the Holy Trinity, but there is also a chapter on regeneration. In a narrow sense, adoption is a strictly legal transaction and, like justification, is a declaration based on the work of Christ on our behalf. But to fully understand the privileges purchased for us by Christ, we need to include that mysterious working of the Holy Spirit by which we are born again—born into the family of God and united to Christ. So through extensive teaching about the work of the Spirit in our salvation, we are taken from the transaction of *adoption* to the ongoing joys of *sonship*.

3. *It is personal*. The author shows how the biblical truth of adoption speaks to life situations, including delicate ones. The book is laced with brief testimonials from people from all kinds of backgrounds and in all manner of personal circumstances. How does adoption into a family where God is our Father impact a single mother? Or someone who has been adopted? Or someone who has adopted children? Dr. Peterson includes all these people. I was particularly pleased that he did not feel constrained to compromise the truth of God as our Father in order to accommodate those whose earthly fathers have failed them. There is sensitivity to such problems, but a poor relationship with a human father does not negate the possibility of relating to God as Father. We all have in our heart a sense of what a father should be. There is a hope deep within all of us that such an ideal father can be found—as indeed we do find him through Christ.

For several years, I was associated with World Harvest Mission, a ministry that includes a renewal program called "Sonship." While teaching Sonship, it was a constant pleasure to watch people be renewed spiritually as they came to "know" not only that God had freed them from the condemnation of sin, but also that he had made them his beloved sons and daughters. I believe this book will have that same effect for many readers, and I am happy to be able to commend it.

STEPHEN E. SMALLMAN

Foreword

*I*n the 1970s, before the years and an accumulation of injuries took their toll, I loved to run along the roads and trails that snake their way across Lookout Mountain. Some afternoons those runs were made even more enjoyable by the company of a fellow runner.

About that same time, I began another journey when I started reflecting on the many family images that the Bible uses to describe you, me, our wonderful God, and how he has drawn us all to each other. Ten years ago, I met Robert Peterson, who was on that same journey, and the path has been more enjoyable ever since.

Part of the joy has been repeatedly discovering new images in the picture of the family of God that the Bible paints. In the following pages, Dr. Peterson spreads some of those images before our eyes. And some of the ways he does it are particularly helpful to God's sons and daughters today.

First, *Adopted by God* is a book written for all of God's children, not just scholars, but it makes use of many of the insights of recent biblical and theological research. In the last twenty-five years, there have been four scholarly books and doctoral dissertations written on these themes. There has also been a marked increase in popular-level articles, sermons, and devotionals on the Christian's sonship and God's fatherhood. However, there have been few books that bring the fruit of that serious study to the broader Christian public. *Adopted by God* helps meet that need. God's children in all our churches will be enriched in their Christian lives by reflecting on these incredible realities.

Second, unlike most popular writers on these themes, Dr. Peterson has committed himself to the difficult task of studying dozens of biblical passages where God uses these family images. This is so obviously necessary, but so seldom done. We all think we know what *father, child,* and *household* mean. Unfortunately, too many writers just bring their own preconceived notions to a couple of biblical passages and paint distorted pictures. Too often those preconceptions have been shaped by their own personal histories and the sociological forces of America, whether those forces are the new trends of the twenty-first century or a longing for the 1950s. What is needed is a commitment to derive biblical meaning from the biblical texts themselves, studied in the context of ancient Palestinian and Mediterranean culture.

Dr. Peterson has helped us start down the right path. Of course, we will not agree with his exegesis of every text. The important thing is that he leads us back to the Bible itself. If we learn nothing else from him, we must learn that only our Father's Word infallibly describes the contours of our Father's family. If God's children are going to be liberated from a whole series of distorted pictures of God as Father, we must go to the Bible itself. And we must not go only to one or two favorite verses. We must go to verse after verse after verse where our Father opens the door to his household and welcomes us in for a closer look.

Third, there has been a great need for studies of the family of God that reflect the incredible breadth of the Bible itself. Today our families touch many parts of our lives. In the ancient world of both the Old Testament and the New Testament, the family was even more significant in a person's life. So it isn't surprising that the Bible uses family images to describe almost every aspect of our individual lives, every category of Christian theology, and every part of our lives together as the church.

This breadth is reflected in the works of writers such as John Calvin. Calvin did not devote any particular section of his *Institutes of the Christian Religion* to adoption. Instead, the family images reappear throughout his writings. An intriguing question is whether the Westminster Confession of Faith, by creating a separate chapter on adoption and grouping all familial themes there, actually de-emphasizes those themes it seeks to emphasize. Minimally, it can be said that Calvin displays the incredible breadth of the Bible in a way that the Westminster Confession does not.

Similarly, the devotional and discipleship literature of recent years has seldom reflected this biblical breadth. More often, there has been a focus on one or two of the familial themes, such as intimacy with God our Father or the liberty of the child of God. Other important parts of the biblical mosaic are eclipsed from view. For example, Jesus' call, "Be ye perfect as your *Father* in heaven is perfect," is seldom mentioned. And many more passages also set forth the responsibility of the Father's children to display their family resemblance (see Deut. 14:1; Mal. 1:6; Matt. 5:9, 16; 21:31; Mark 3:35; Luke 6:35–36; Rom. 8:12–15; Eph. 5:1; Phil. 2:14–15; Heb. 2:11–17; 1 Peter 1:14–15; 1 John 2:29–3:3).

Adopted by God helps us take a crucial step beyond accepting simplistic definitions of God's fatherhood, sonship, and adoption. It helps us see that the biblical texture of these themes is much more intricately woven. For example, Dr. Peterson reminds us that assurance of being God's child involves cultivating the family resemblance through obedience and suffering. Similarly, one of the Father's great gifts is to discipline his children.

As Robert Peterson and I have been journeying through the riches of the family of God, I've become more and more convinced of five things, all reflected in this book. First, God's children really can be enriched by joining us on this journey. Second, we must all go to the Bible, because that is where our Father has revealed what his family will look like. Third, the biblical mosaic of the family of God is carefully nuanced and touches all of life and theology. Fourth, we have much further to go in our exploration of these glorious riches, and we need others to help us. Fifth, even though Robert Peterson and I have often taken different paths in exploring these themes, it is a joy to search the family riches with a brother.

ALLEN MAWHINNEY

Acknowledgments

I am grateful to the following friends and family members for their part in the completion of this work:

Allen Mawhinney, for inspiration, encouragement, and mentoring in the biblical pictures of the family of God.

David Farley, Mike Graham, Rod Jamison, Chris Morgan, Laura Muckerman, Bob O'Bannon, Diane Preston, Roger Price, Neil Williams, and Wes Zell, for taking time from busy schedules to read the manuscript and make comments. Special thanks are due Wes for compiling the subject index.

Mary Pat, for her constant love and faithfulness. Robby, Matthew, Curtis, and David, for caring for and praying for me.

Barbara Lerch, for encouragement; Jim Scott, for careful copy editing; and Thom Notaro, for wise counsel.

P&R Publishing, for unwavering commitment to the Word of God in an age of increasing compromise.

Why Consider Adoption?

*D*ying Woman's Children Advertise for New Family."
So ran the headline for an Associated Press story
from London on February 13, 1998. Ten-year-old British
twins, whose mother was dying of cancer, placed an ad in
their local newspaper, *The Oxford Mail*, that ran, "Kids and
dogs for hire. Life term contract. Sad gits [losers] need not
apply." The story continued:

> Lauren and Ashton Mills made their appeal in the
> "Situations Vacant" column of Wednesday's *Mail*
> with the full approval of their mother, Tobi, 43. A
> single mother, Tobi has been diagnosed with breast
> cancer that later spread to her liver. By Thursday
> thousands of potential foster families had re-
> sponded to the twins' plea. . . . The twins said that
> the ad was "a bit of fun" that made their mother
> laugh but stressed that the point was serious. "We
> both know that soon we are going to need some-
> one to be our new mum and dad," Ashton told *The
> Sun*, Britain's largest newspaper. "I want somebody
> who will listen to me, someone who doesn't lose

their temper for no reason. I don't want them to be as strict as Mum can be."

All readers can empathize with Lauren's and Ashton's desire for a loving, stable family. Whether our childhood was very happy, very sad, or somewhere in between, we all know the joys and sorrows of family life. In addition, every one of us who has trusted Christ as Lord and Savior is part of another family—the family of God. All believers have a heavenly Father, a unique older Brother, and many brothers and sisters. We have family privileges and responsibilities, whether or not we are fully aware of them. The purpose of this book is to make us more aware of the privileges of being in the family of God—along with the attendant responsibilities. As a result, we will be better able to glorify our Father who is in heaven and to live on earth as befits the sons and daughters of the living God.

A good way to begin is by asking, Why consider adoption? Many good answers could be given to this question, but I will offer three. We should consider adoption because of:

> *The needs of human hearts*
> *Neglect by Christian theologians*
> *The incredible richness of God's grace*

The Needs of Human Hearts

In 1884, a liberal periodical chose as its name *The Christian Century,* hoping that the twentieth century would be just that. Sadly, after many terrible wars, including two world wars, and after unspeakable genocide in various countries, the optimistic hopes have been dashed.

During the early years of a new millennium, will we hear similar expressions of optimism? If we do, will we believe them? Many words characterize our society today. Although a complete list would include positive words, I will select three that point to deep needs—needs that can be met fully only by knowing God as heavenly Father.[1]

BIGOTRY

It is shocking that at the end of a century that promised to promote more goodwill for all people, we hear of neo-Nazi skinheads in Europe attacking people simply because they are "different," and read news reports of horrible racial crimes committed in America. I cannot get out of my mind the story of James Byrd Jr., the black man in Texas murdered by racist whites who dragged him to his death behind their pickup truck. At a time when many predicted that bigotry would be a thing of the past, sadly, it is still very much alive. This does not bode well for an America that will be marked by even greater racial, economic, and age diversity in the years ahead.

Plainly, American believers need to demonstrate the unity of the family of God. And a watching world needs to see churches where there is neither rich nor poor, neither black, nor yellow, nor white, neither male nor female, neither young nor old, but where brothers and sisters in Christ are truly one in Christ Jesus.

LONELINESS

Our age is marked by a sense of isolation. I will mention only two causes of this: technology and divorce. Incredible advances in communication and transportation technologies have greatly improved modern life. Those same ad-

3

vances, however, have also compounded our sense of lone-liness, because technology sometimes has reduced our inti-macy with other human beings. For example, most children spend much more time with TVs, VCRs, and computers than they do with their parents and siblings.

Technology, however, is not the chief source of loneli-ness. Divorce is. As more adults practice what amounts to serial polygamy, family members are alienated from one an-other. Men, women, and, above all, children are hurting. They feel so alone. All are affected by the shattering of the American family. How many extended families do you know that are untouched by divorce? And the immediate fu-ture shows no sign that our selfishness will suddenly come to a halt. Rather, we are probably in for greater sorrow.

People hurt by the ravages of divorce need the fellow-ship of a heavenly Father and the fellowship of his daughters and sons. They need to know that they have a Father in heaven who loves them with an everlasting love, who can be trusted and who will not betray them. And we who know this Father must love them and introduce them to his family.

INSECURITY

For many people today, the old certainties are gone for-ever. They no longer embrace the concept of absolute truth; the very idea is out of fashion. In its place is the idea of things being true for you or for me. Along with this intel-lectual relativism comes moral relativism. In the minds of many, there are no longer absolute standards of right and wrong. Instead, matters are considered more or less appro-priate, depending upon a variety of factors, not the least of which is personal happiness.

Make no mistake about it—this intellectual and moral

relativism exacts a heavy toll. Indeed, many postmoderns are insecure. They need to belong, but are afraid to trust and uncertain whom to trust. Friends and neighbors, people just like us, join cults, partially because the groups promise to provide love, security, and a sense of belonging. Such knowledge is alarming.

The only lasting security in this life comes from a personal knowledge of the Son of God, who loved us and gave himself for us. Everyone else will disappoint us at times, and we will disappoint others. But there is One who does not disappoint any who believe that he died and rose again to rescue them from their sins. True security is found in him, for he grants to repentant sinners the forgiveness of sins, eternal life, and a place in the family of God.

In summary, because our age is characterized by bigotry, loneliness, and insecurity, we who live in it need the unity of the family of God, the fellowship of a heavenly Father, and the security that comes from knowing the Son of God. In a word, we need to learn about and live out our sonship, as my friend Mark underscores:

> The doctrine of adoption is one of the most precious doctrines we have as children of God. Just to be called "children of God" is such a wonderful blessing. Because I am now in God's family, I have a new relationship with God. No longer is he just a being far away; now he is my Father. What a tender relationship that is! I really belong in God's family. The Holy Spirit says to me, "Mark, you belong here. You are part of the family." In a day when people feel alone and families are so broken, what a wonderful gift this is. Adoption is indeed a precious truth for me.

Neglect by Christian Theologians

Our problems are compounded because those to whom we might look for help have ignored the greatest source of help. The church's teachers and theologians have devoted little attention to the Bible's teaching on adoption. There are exceptions: Calvin had much to say about adoption in his famous *Institutes of the Christian Religion*. Scottish and Southern Presbyterian theologians have done some good work. Especially worthy of commendation is Sinclair Ferguson's *Children of the Living God*.[2]

Such works, however, are rare. Following Francis Turretin, most Protestant writers have placed adoption under justification and paid little attention to it. Charles Hodge, in his monumental *Systematic Theology*, devotes only one-half of a page to adoption out of more than 2,200 pages (vol. 3, pp. 164–65)! Louis Berkhof, in his *Systematic Theology*, devotes only one page out of 700 to the topic (pp. 515–16). Anthony Hoekema, in *Saved by Grace*, treats adoption in two and one-half pages out of 256 (pp. 185–87). I have not chosen these books at random; they are the textbooks I read in seminary (Hodge) and use in my teaching (Berkhof and Hoekema). Plainly, some of the church's leading teachers have neglected the subject of sonship.

Curiously, when theologians do mention adoption, they do so in different contexts. The three writers mentioned above all treat it as an aspect of justification. The great Dutch theologian Abraham Kuyper wrote of it in connection with regeneration. The American Presbyterian theologian J. Oliver Buswell Jr., placed adoption under glorification. Why the confusion? There are at least two reasons.

First, theologians differ as to where to place adoption in relation to other doctrines because they regard it as an afterthought, hardly deserving attention in its own right. Second, the three positions mentioned above, tying adoption to justification, regeneration, and glorification, respectively, are all partially correct. The instincts of Berkhof, Kuyper, and Buswell were accurate. Adoption, properly considered, overlaps these other three doctrines and more. That is, adoption is an overarching way of viewing the Christian faith. Adoption pertains to the beginning of salvation, the Christian life, and the resurrection of the dead.

Thankfully, not everyone has neglected the study of adoption. The framers of the Heidelberg Catechism asked and wisely answered question 33: "Why is he called God's 'only Son' when we also are God's children? Because Christ alone is the eternal, natural Son of God. We, however, are adopted children of God—adopted by grace through Christ." And the Puritans who drafted the Westminster standards included a small chapter on adoption in the Confession of Faith (chapter 12), and answered Shorter Catechism question 34 as follows: "Adoption is an act of God's free grace, whereby we are received into the number, and have a right to all the privileges, of the sons of God." One reason we study sonship is to remedy past neglect.

The Incredible Richness of God's Grace

Neither the needs of moderns nor the neglect of theologians is the most important reason to study adoption. That distinction belongs to the incredible richness of God's grace that is revealed in the doctrine of sonship. This richness is helpfully viewed from the perspective of the panorama of God's grace. Salvation is presented in Scripture as God's gracious work from beginning to end. He plans, accomplishes, applies, and consummates redemption.

Salvation was planned by the Trinity, especially by God the Father, in choosing people for salvation before the creation of the world. Salvation was accomplished by the Trinity, especially by God the Son, in his death and resurrection. Salvation is applied by the Trinity, especially by God the Holy Spirit, when he brings grace to bear on the lives of human beings. Salvation will be consummated by the Trinity—Father, Son, and Holy Spirit—in the resurrection of the dead for life in the new heavens and new earth. In sum, it is helpful for us to view redemption as planned, accomplished, applied, and consummated. Scripture itself talks about these four aspects of salvation in terms of sonship.

SALVATION PLANNED

"In love [the Father] predestined us to be adopted as his sons through Jesus Christ" (Eph. 1:4–5). Here is the source of tremendous comfort: our sonship was planned by the Father before he made the worlds. He loved us and chose to include us in his family before time. How dear we are to him and how dear he should be to us. Joy's prayer poignantly underscores this truth:

> Dear Father, as I awaited the adoption of my first grandchild on the other side of the world last year, I didn't know if I would love her as I knew I would a child my daughter had given birth to. I didn't know what she'd be like or look like, if she'd be healthy or not. But as I prayed for her all these months, you filled my heart so full of love for her that the day I first saw her I would have given her anything. I know that's just a glimpse of how much you love me

and have already given me everything. Thank you for allowing me to see this. Amen, Joy.

SALVATION ACCOMPLISHED

"When the time had fully come, God sent his Son, born of a woman, born under law, to redeem those under law, that we might receive the full rights of sons" (Gal. 4:4–5). The work of Christ, portrayed in terms of adoption, is a redemption. Christ bore the curse of the law to redeem those who were slaves to sin (Gal. 3:13). Here is great cause for rejoicing. Jesus, the unique Son of God, has died to set us free from bondage to sin. We do not have to live as slaves to sin any longer. Sin's stranglehold over our lives has been broken. The glory belongs to the crucified and risen Son, and his victory belongs to us. We need to learn more about the freedom that is ours as daughters and sons of God.

SALVATION APPLIED

"For you did not receive a spirit that makes you a slave again to fear, but you received the Spirit of sonship. And by him we cry, '*Abba,* Father'" (Rom. 8:15). Adoption is another way of speaking of the application of salvation. God the Holy Spirit graciously opens our hearts so that we freely accept the Son of God as he is offered in the gospel. The Spirit gives us the gift of saving faith and enables us to cry out to God in truth, "*Abba,* Father." Such knowledge strengthens us. Our childlike cry of saving faith is a reflex action to the grace of the Holy Spirit that we have already received.

How much God loves us, his children, to deal with us so graciously! When we were slaves to the devil, God gave us his Spirit so we might become his children. Perhaps your human father is a wonderful example of God's fatherhood, and perhaps not. Regardless, if you believe in Christ, you have a Father in heaven who delights in you and who has saved you freely by his grace. And that should make a difference in your life. Consider the testimony of major league pitcher Paul Byrd, given in August 1999:

> Phillies pitcher Paul Byrd is a devout Christian who happens to lead the National League with 13 hit batsmen. Former Brave Byrd is close pals with Atlanta catcher Eddie Perez, who has been repeatedly plunked, nicked and banged up since taking over for the injured Javy Lopez this summer. So Perez was already in a foul mood when Byrd hit him with a fastball in the third inning of a July 30 game at Turner Field. He barked at Byrd, and both benches emptied, though nobody threw any punches.
>
> In the fourth, Atlanta's John Smoltz retaliated by plunking Alex Arias. Umpire Jerry Meals ejected Smoltz, which further annoyed Perez. Reliever Russ Springer replaced Smoltz, Byrd stepped to the plate, and that's when all heck broke loose. The mild-mannered 185-pound Byrd told Perez that he hadn't meant to hit him the inning before. But the burly catcher wasn't buying it. He shoved Byrd and smacked him on the head with his catcher's mitt. The two fought as Meals stepped aside, the benches cleared again and what one witness calls "a huge angry pig-pile" formed on the ground around home plate.
>
> Byrd and Perez were face-to-face at the bottom of the pile. "The Lord Jesus is my daddy," Byrd

yelled, "and he takes care of his children! He knows I wasn't trying to hit you. He's going to take care of me, so you better be careful with me."

The surprised Perez felt his anger melt away. "I said, 'Stay with me, Birdie. I'll help you,'" he says.

"Eddie couldn't get off me fast enough," says Byrd. "It was like I was on fire."

Meals tossed Perez after the fight. Byrd stayed in the game and won it to run his record to 12–6, then insisted he is no headhunter. "It's not my intention to hit people," he said, "but the Lord blessed me with a short right arm and an 85 mile-an-hour fastball. I have to throw inside."

Perez laughed when he heard that. "Yeah," he said, "but not at my elbow."[3]

SALVATION CONSUMMATED

"The creation waits in eager expectation for the sons of God to be revealed" (Rom. 8:19). Thanks to the Son of God, we are center stage in God's plan. The creation takes a back seat to us. It longs for our final salvation, because in that day the creation too will get in on the blessings—our blessings. Our full identity will be made known only when Jesus returns. Then it will be revealed what beautiful sons and daughters of God he has made us. In the meantime, we "groan inwardly as we wait eagerly for our adoption as sons, the redemption of our bodies" (Rom. 8:23). This glorious expectation should inspire great hope within us. One day God will give us the final installment of our sonship. Every part of us will be completely redeemed, including our bodies. God will equip us to enter into our full inheritance on the new earth. Then he will conform us fully to the likeness of his Son (Rom. 8:29). Such thoughts are too wonderful for us; we can hardly take them in.

We marvel at the grace of God, who has planned, accomplished, and applied and will yet consummate our adoption. We can rejoice with Tami:

> Until looking closely at adoption, I never really understood it. Adoption just seemed like a foreign concept to which I could not relate! Now, however, I understand that I truly am one of God's children. Even though both of my parents here are not believers, my Father in heaven is! It's okay now that my parents don't or can't understand me and the decisions I make when it comes to Christianity. God does. I have an eternal parent who will never leave me. And, whose love is not conditional. That's pretty cool!

Indeed, God's sonship is divine! The rest of this book will explore the joy of knowing God as our heavenly Father.

Is Adoption in
the Old Testament?

*A*t first blush, the New Testament appears to send contradictory signals about adoption in the Old Testament. In Romans 9:4–5, Paul lists blessings that God bestowed upon the people of Israel:

> Theirs is the adoption as sons; theirs the divine glory, the covenants, the receiving of the law, the temple worship and the promises. Theirs are the patriarchs, and from them is traced the human ancestry of Christ, who is God over all, forever praised! Amen.

This is an imposing list, and its last item is plainly the greatest: Christ. But notice what Paul mentions first: adoption. By contrast, in Galatians 4:1–3, Paul seems to regard Old Testament adoption as a form of second-class spiritual citizenship: "When we were children"—Paul speaks of Jews under the old covenant—"we were in slavery." Israel's sonship was characterized by immaturity and even bondage. How, then, are we to regard adoption in the Old Testament? Is it a great blessing or a second-rate one?

We can reconcile the apparent contradiction by viewing Old Testament Israel's sonship from two perspectives: looking around and looking back. First, as we look around from the vantage point of the ancient Near East, Israel's adoption by God was a great benefit. Adoption set Israel apart from the idolatry of its pagan neighbors. To belong to the only nation adopted by God was a great blessing. Second, we can consider Israel's sonship by looking back from the New Testament. From this vantage point, Israel's adoption was incomplete; the bestowal of the full status of adult sonship depended on the unique Son's coming to do his saving work. Adoption in its fullest sense, therefore, is a New Testament reality.

This chapter will consider:

> God as father in the Old Testament
> "God's son" in the Old Testament[1]

God as Father in the Old Testament

If we examine the words with which the Old Testament speaks of the family of God, the first thing that strikes us is how infrequently the word *father* is applied to God. The Old Testament calls God "father" only fifteen times, a small number compared to the tally of 118 for the gospel of John alone. Why does the Old Testament hesitate to call God "father"? We can suggest an answer: because of the idolatry of Israel's neighbors. Many ancient peoples called God "father" in an impure sense. The Egyptians and Mesopotamians believed in a plurality of gods and arranged them by genealogy. Thus, to call a deity "father" meant that he was the source of the other gods. He was thought to have consorted with a female deity to produce divine offspring. In this way, the pantheon arose.

Given this false idea of divine fatherhood, it is not surprising that ancient Near Eastern nations used the expression _son of god_ in error, too. In Egypt, the pharaoh was regarded as the god Horus, the son of the gods Osiris and Isis. The pharaoh was thus thought to be a god begotten by a god. In Egypt, therefore, the sonship of the king was by begetting. In Mesopotamia, by contrast, the kings were not regarded as divine, but were thought to be great men chosen and installed by the gods as their representatives. Theirs was a case of royal sonship by adoption.

The two dominant ancient Near Eastern cultures contemporary with Israel's, the Egyptian and the Mesopotamian, then, understood divine fatherhood and human sonship within a framework of polytheism. In light of this background, we can readily understand the reticence of God to call himself "father" in the Old Testament. Too many false connotations attached themselves to that term. In light of the idolatrous background, the best name for God in the Old Testament was not Father, nor the Trinity, but One, the living and true God in distinction from the false gods of the nations. Sadly, however, Israel, who imitated her neighbors' sins, called idols "father" in a sinful sense, too. God chastens the rebellious nation in Jeremiah 2:27–28:

> They say to wood, "You are my father," and to stone, "You gave me birth." They have turned their backs to me and not their faces; yet when they are in trouble, they say, "Come and save us!" Where then are the gods you made for yourselves? Let them come if they can save you when you are in trouble! For you have as many gods as you have towns, O Judah.

When God does call himself "father" in the Old Testament, the term almost always refers to him as Savior rather than Creator. A good example occurs in Isaiah 63:16, where the prophet declares, "But you are our Father, though Abraham does not know us or Israel acknowledge us; you, O LORD, are our Father, our Redeemer from of old is your name." Again, the reason why God is called "Father, our Redeemer," and not "Father, our Creator," is to avoid confusion with contemporary errors. The Old Testament, from its first chapter onward, asserts clearly and frequently that God is the Creator, but it reserves the word *father* to speak of God as he delivers his people from Egypt.

The past century has witnessed an error related to the ancient ones that Israel's prophets opposed in God's name. The old liberalism proudly proclaimed the universal fatherhood of God and the universal brotherhood of man. That is, God is everyone's Father, and all human beings are brothers and sisters. This was one way that liberalism distorted the gospel. If God is already our Father, then we don't need to be redeemed, we don't need an atonement, and we don't need to trust Christ as our substitute.

In fact, according to Scripture, God *is* everyone's Father by creation; this is a minor chord in the New Testament symphony (Acts 17:28; James 1:17). But it is wrong to say simply that God is everyone's Father and just leave it at that. Chiefly, he is Father by virtue of redemption, and in this regard all are not his children. Rather, many are children of their father, the devil. They need to be redeemed and become children of God by faith in the unique Son of God (1 John 3:10; Gal. 4:4, 7).

The Bible is God's instrument to counter errors, both ancient and modern. This truth is as important today as at any time in church history. Our culture is poisoned by false teaching from many sources, including the New Age movement, Mormonism, Jehovah's Witnesses, and other cults. What is the divine antidote to this poison? If our church, our families, and our children are to stand fast against the attacks of the Evil One, we must take up "the sword of the Spirit, which is the word of God" (Eph. 6:17).

How are we to learn the Word of God? I will mention two ways. First, by supporting Sunday school. Make sure your children are there—and go yourself. If you have the gift of teaching, then take your turn to teach. You and your students will benefit. Second, fathers, spend time around the dinner table reading the Bible to your family. The spiritual nurture of your children is not primarily the responsibility of the church, the Christian school, or the youth pastor—it is the responsibility of you and your wife. I give God the glory that our sons have learned to think in a Christian manner in our family times of Bible reading and discussion following our evening meal. Single mothers, do not be discouraged. God will be Father and husband to you. Trust him for strength and wisdom and lead your children in devotions at the dinner table or at bedtime. Your heavenly Father will work through you to bless them.

"God's Son" in the Old Testament

Who is God's son in the Old Testament? The answer to this question will help us to understand the New Testament idea of adoption. The Old Testament gives three answers:

The nation of Israel
The king of Israel
Individual Israelites

17

THE NATION OF ISRAEL

Most frequently, God's son is the nation of Israel. A good example is found in Deuteronomy 32:6: "Is this the way you repay the LORD, O foolish and unwise people? Is he not your Father, your Creator, who made you and formed you?" Here God is Israel's father, and Israel is God's son. But doesn't this text refer to God as Creator, rather than Redeemer? Yes, the verse does use the language of creation, but it employs this language in reference to God's redemption of the nation from Egypt, as the following verses indicate. God brought Israel into being—he created her, so to speak—by loving, protecting, and leading her.

> For the LORD's portion is his people, Jacob his allotted inheritance. In a desert land he found him, in a barren and howling waste. He shielded him and cared for him; he guarded him as the apple of his eye, like an eagle that stirs up its nest and hovers over its young, that spreads its wings to catch them and carries them on its pinions. The LORD alone led him; no foreign god was with him. (Deut. 32:9–12)

Verse 15 reinforces the conclusion that Moses uses the language of creation to tell of Israel's redemption: "Jeshurun grew fat and kicked; filled with food, he became heavy and sleek. He abandoned the God who made him and rejected the Rock his Savior."

Hosea also speaks of Israel as God's son:

> When Israel was a child, I loved him, and out of Egypt I called my son. . . . It was I who taught Ephraim to walk, taking them by the arms; but they

did not realize it was I who healed them. I led them with cords of human kindness, with ties of love; I lifted the yoke from their neck and bent down to feed them. (Hos. 11:1, 3–4)

This passage helps us understand sonship in a number of ways. First, note that adoption is based on redemption: "Out of Egypt I called my son." Second, notice the combination of love and sonship: "When Israel was a child, I loved him." We will hear echoes of these principles in the New Testament. Third, the New Testament itself quotes Hosea 11:1. In Matthew 2:15, we learn that when Joseph took the baby Jesus to Egypt, out of harm's way in Judea, his action "fulfilled what the Lord had said through the prophet: 'Out of Egypt I called my son.'" Here Matthew applies to Christ an Old Testament statement of Israel's sonship. So who is the "son" referred to in Hosea 11:1—Israel or Christ? Clearly, in its original context, Hosea 11:1 speaks of the nation of Israel, God's chosen people, redeemed from Egyptian bondage, as his son. But, just as clearly, Matthew says that the Hosea text was "fulfilled" when Joseph took Jesus and Mary to Egypt for a time. How are we to put these facts together?

Here is the likely solution. Christ came as the Promised One, an individual Israelite who accomplished on behalf of the nation what it could not do for itself. "Jesus Christ the son of David, the son of Abraham" (Matt. 1:1), embodied Israel in himself. In place of the twelve tribes, he chose twelve disciples. As Israel was brought out of Egypt, so was he (Matt. 2:14–15). As the nation was tempted in the wilderness, so was he (Matt. 4:1–11). As God gave the nation the Ten Commandments, so he gave the people a new law (the

Sermon on the Mount, Matt. 5–7). Most importantly, as Israel was delivered by the Exodus, so he accomplished *the* great redemptive deed in his death and resurrection. In Luke's version of the Transfiguration, Moses and Elijah appear with Jesus on the mount, and they speak "about his departure, which he was about to bring to fulfillment at Jerusalem" (Luke 9:31). The Greek word translated "departure" is *exodos.* The Son of God would fulfill his "exodus" by going to the cross. The typology is unmistakable. The deliverance from Egypt was a type of Jesus' crucifixion. The Old Testament nation, God's son, therefore, is concentrated in one Israelite, Jesus Christ, who is the Son of God *par excellence.*

Our study of God's son in the Old Testament highlights the grace of God for us today. It is wonderful to contemplate that, from the beginning, God chose one nation from all the rest, Israel, and planned to bring one Israelite from that nation. This individual would accomplish what the nation could never do for itself. He would redeem Israel—and more! He would rescue not only believing Jews, but also Gentiles who would put their trust in him. This means that God planned our salvation from of old. Whenever we read of Israel in the Old Testament, therefore, we are reminded of God's grace, because all along he had in mind to bring our Savior from Israel. From God's son Israel, God brought God's Son Jesus Christ, so that we would become God's sons and daughters through faith in him. Surely our Father in heaven loves us and made great provision to include us in his family.

THE KING OF ISRAEL

God's son in the Old Testament is sometimes the king of Israel. In 2 Samuel 7, God denies David's request to build a house (a temple) for him, and informs him that his son will build that house instead. Through Nathan the prophet, God promises to establish a "house" (a dynasty) for King David:

> The LORD declares to you that the LORD himself will establish a house for you: When your days are over and you rest with your fathers, I will raise up your offspring to succeed you, who will come from your own body, and I will establish his kingdom. He is the one who will build a house for my Name, and I will establish the throne of his kingdom forever. I will be his father, and he will be my son. . . . Your house and your kingdom will endure forever before me; your throne will be established forever. (2 Sam. 7:11–14, 16)

When God pledges to bring a royal dynasty from David's loins, he uses family language. Concerning Solomon and his descendants, God promises, "I will be his father, and he will be my son." Here, God's "son" is not the nation as a whole, but the king who will carry on David's line.

The New Testament applies 2 Samuel 7:14 to Christ. Hebrews 1 contrasts the Son of God with the angels: "For to which of the angels did God ever say, 'You are my Son; today I have become your Father'? Or again, 'I will be his Father, and he will be my Son'?" (Heb. 1:5). Here the writer to the Hebrews applies to Christ the words of Psalm 2:7 and 2 Samuel 7:14. Our concern is with the latter. The paternal relationship between God the Father and the Lord Jesus Christ is expressed in the words of that passage, "I will be his father, and he will be my son." This is fitting in Hebrews 1, for this chapter sets forth Christ in his threefold office as prophet (v. 2), priest (v. 3), and, chiefly, king. As a king, he has a "throne," a "scepter," and a "kingdom" (v. 8). As the crucified and risen one, "he sat down at the right hand of the Majesty in heaven" (v. 3). From here, the supreme location of honor and authority, the unique Son rules with his Father. So, in the end, the king who will reign forever on David's throne is not Solomon, nor any other of David's merely human descendants, but the incomparable descendant of David, the divine Son of God, Jesus Christ.

Here is a source of great comfort for the people of God. Our Savior Jesus Christ sits at the Father's right hand. He rules over all. Although there is terrible wickedness on the earth, nothing is beyond his control. King Jesus watches over us, armed with "all authority in heaven and on earth" (Matt. 28:18). John Calvin trumpeted the corporate and individual benefits of Jesus' royal office:

> Therefore, whenever we hear of Christ as armed with eternal power, let us remember that the perpetuity of the church is secure in this protection. . . . Hence it follows that the devil, with all the resources of the world, can never destroy the church, founded as it is on the eternal throne of Christ.
>
> . . . In like manner, Christ enriches his people with all things necessary for the eternal salvation of souls and fortifies them with courage to stand unconquerable against all the assaults of spiritual enemies. . . .
>
> . . . Our King will never leave us destitute, but will provide for our needs until, our warfare ended, we are called to triumph.[2]

Thus we see that when the Old Testament speaks of the nation of Israel or the king of Israel as God's son, it points ultimately to Christ.

INDIVIDUAL ISRAELITES

In the Old Testament, God's "son" is sometimes an individual Israelite. For example, in Proverbs 3:11–12, we read, "My son, do not despise the LORD's discipline and do not resent his rebuke, because the LORD disciplines those he loves, as a father the son he delights in." This text is quoted in Hebrews 12:5–6, where the writer wants to establish the fact that God's discipline of Christians is a proof of sonship and a sign of God's love.

The discipline spoken of in Hebrews, taken in its historical setting, is God's allowing them to suffer for their faith. God disciplines his children by calling them to persevere in the face of difficult trials. How about you? Are you going through hard times right now? Are you enduring difficulties that you would rather not endure? If so, count them as tokens of your heavenly Father's love. Regard them as paternal discipline. The good news is that the sovereign God of the universe is your Father. He loves you dearly and has brought into your life the struggles that he knows will draw you close to him.

> How much more should we submit to the Father of our spirits and live! . . . God disciplines us for our good, that we may share in his holiness. No discipline seems pleasant at the time, but painful. Later on, however, it produces a harvest of righteousness and peace for those who have been trained by it. (Heb. 12:9–11)

Our second example is Psalm 103. Verse 8 repeats the glorious Old Testament refrain, "The LORD is compassionate and gracious, slow to anger, abounding in love." Then the psalm approaches a New Testament conception of grace when it declares, "He does not treat us as our sins deserve or repay us according to our iniquities" (v. 10). Next it appeals to the grand scale of God's world to illustrate his incomparable love and the greatness of his forgiveness: "For as high as the heavens are above the earth, so great is his love for those who fear him; as far as the east is from the west, so far has he removed our transgressions from us" (vv. 11–12). Finally, verse 13 proclaims, "As a father has compassion on his children, so the LORD has compassion on those who fear him." The psalmist likens God's love for his obedient people to that of a caring father for his children.

Ron Dayne, winner of the 1999 Heisman Trophy, an award given annually to the best collegiate football player, knows just such a father figure. After Dayne's parents divorced when he was fifteen, he was taken into the family of his uncle, Pentecostal minister Rob Reid. Dayne's tribute to his uncle reminds me of what Psalm 103:13 says about the compassionate father:

> I began to think about you and the Heisman Trophy.
>
> I remember when I first came to live with you and Aunt Deb. The first thing we did was have a family meeting; all of us were sitting around the kitchen table, you, Aunt Deb, Rob Jr., Jaquay and Joel. You announced that no one was going to get any new clothes until I had as many outfits as everybody else. Well, Joel did not care about clothes then, Jaquay wore uniforms to school, but Rob got

"swole." Rob had so many clothes it was ridiculous. And soon after that, I did too. For that Uncle Rob, you win the Heisman.

I remember you traveling with me on my college visits to Wisconsin and Ohio State. We hated Ohio State, didn't we, Uncle Rob? That is why we beat them so badly last week. For traveling with me and helping me make the right decision, you win the Heisman.

Uncle Rob, you go see Rob play football in Virginia; you go see Jaquay run track in Virginia; but you still come out to Wisconsin to see me, too. For that Uncle Rob, you win the Heisman.

And when you do come to Wisconsin, you slip one or two hundred dollar bills in my hand. For that Uncle Rob, YOU REALLY WIN THE HEISMAN.

When Rob left for college, I started to try some of our tricks, by myself, and got caught every time. We never got caught when Rob was home. Like when I squeezed out of the bathroom window one night to see a girl—when I tried to get back in at 1:00 a.m., you had locked that window and the rest of the windows in the house. I had to ring that doorbell and look in your face. You never said a word. You didn't have to. For that Uncle Rob, you win the Heisman.

Uncle Rob, for never making me feel like a nephew, but always making me feel like a SON, for that Uncle Rob, you win the Heisman.[3]

In summary, whether God's son in the Old Testament is Israel, the king, or an individual Israelite, we keep returning to the New Testament. This is fitting, for the doctrine of adoption is fully developed in the New Testament, not the Old. It is to the New Testament that we now turn, specifically to the letters of the apostle Paul, who wrote the most on adoption. In the next chapter, we will consider why people need to be adopted by God.

3

Slaves of Sin No More!

I happen actually to have been adopted as an infant, so the doctrine of adoption is especially real to me. Briefly, it means that while I was without a future, a hope, even a family to belong to, somebody gave me all of these and more. And this was done, not because of anything I could ever give back in return for such a gift, but just because my parents wanted—even needed—to express their love to someone. Likewise, according to the Word of God, God the Father chose me and adopted me, so he could love me. I will never fully understand why my parents or God chose me. But I am forever humbled and just plain amazed that they did.

Patrick's words move us. We rejoice with him when he recalls his adoption by his parents. We understand salvation better when he presents his physical adoption as a picture of spiritual sonship. One reason that his story keeps our attention is that he frankly shares his need for adoption: "I was without a future, a hope, even a family to belong to." This suggests an important question: What is *our* need for adoption by God the Father?

Pictures of Salvation

It is helpful to consider our need for adoption in light of the Bible's various pictures of salvation. The Scriptures paint salvation in bright hues: salvation is justification, sanctification, regeneration, calling, conversion, union with Christ, and adoption. Why does God use so many images to portray the reality of our salvation? The multiplicity of the pictures of salvation corresponds to the greatness of our need. That is, to each of these images corresponds a picture of our need for salvation. Salvation is understood properly only in light of our need for it. We only appreciate the remedy when we are aware of the disease. Let's consider the following six images of salvation. For each, let's try to come up with the corresponding image of our need.

PICTURE OF SALVATION	PICTURE OF NEED
Justification	?
Sanctification	?
Regeneration	?
Calling	?
Conversion	?
Union with Christ	?

When we fill in the chart correctly, and add adoption to it, it looks like this:

PICTURE OF SALVATION	PICTURE OF NEED
Justification	Condemnation
Sanctification	Contamination
Regeneration	Death
Calling	Deafness

Conversion	Wandering away from God
Union with Christ	Separation from Christ
Adoption	?

Adoption is another way of talking about salvation, this time using a family image. What is the picture of our need that corresponds to salvation when it is viewed as adoption? When I ask this question in adult Sunday school classes, people frequently reply, "We were orphans." While this answer is partially correct, in reality our plight was much worse.

Before God the Father adopted us as his sons and daughters in Christ, we were not merely orphans—we were slaves. That is why Paul describes a Christian as "no longer a slave, but a son" (Gal. 4:7). And that explains the contrast in Romans 8:15, "For you did not receive a spirit that makes you a slave again to fear, but you received the Spirit of sonship." Galatians 4:3 specifies, "We were in slavery under the basic principles of the world." What are "the basic principles of the world" (RSV: "the elemental spirits of the universe"; NASB: "the elemental things of the world") that held us in chains before Christ set us free? To answer this question, we must explore the four passages that describe the state of bondage out of which we were adopted: Colossians 2:8, Colossians 2:20–21, Galatians 4:3, and Galatians 4:8–11.

"The Basic Principles of This World"

In Colossians 2:8, Paul warns, "See to it that no one takes you captive through hollow and deceptive philosophy, which depends on human tradition and *the basic principles of this world* rather than on Christ." The "basic principles

29

of this world" (*stoicheia tou kosmou*) lie behind philosophies that are opposed to Christ. Do they signify worldly wisdom or perhaps the powers of darkness that inspire it?

In Colossians 2:20–21, Paul warns against a false asceticism, the idea that holiness is achieved through the denial of the physical appetites. "Since you died with Christ to *the basic principles of this world*, why, as though you still belonged to it, do you submit to its rules: 'Do not handle! Do not taste! Do not touch!'?" When Christians are united to Christ, they die to "the basic principles of this world." Here "the basic principles" are associated with asceticism. Once more, these "principles" could be understood as either ungodly ideas or the realm of spiritual forces that spawn them.

In Colossians, then, "the basic principles, the elements, of this world" generate false ideas and ungodly living. Are these "basic principles" worldly wisdom or something more sinister—"the spiritual forces of evil in the heavenly realms" (Eph. 6:12)? In either case, this much is clear: Christ has broken the power of "the basic principles of this world" over his people, although in ignorance they can return to them.

What about the two passages in Galatians? Paul says in Galatians 4:8–11,

> Formerly, when you did not know God, you were slaves to those who by nature are not gods. But now that you know God—or rather are known by God—how is it that you are turning back to those weak and miserable *principles*? Do you wish to be enslaved by them all over again? You are observing special days and months and seasons and years! I fear for you, that somehow I have wasted my efforts on you.

Paul gives God the glory for the conversion of the Galatians. He explains that when they came to know God, they were already "known by God." That is, God, not they, initiated their salvation. Note Paul's distinction between "those who by nature are not gods" (Gal. 4:8) and the God who knew the Galatians (v. 9). For the Gentiles to be enslaved by false gods is to be under the control of "the basic principles of this world," here called "those weak and miserable *principles* [*stoicheia*]" (v. 9). In this passage, the "principles" in view seem to be more than ungodly ideas; they are "those who by nature are not gods," that is, demons.

Remarkably (and here we return to our starting place), in Galatians 4:3, Paul says of the Jews before their conversion to Christ, "So also, when we were children, we were in slavery under the basic principles of the world." The apostle surprises us. He says that the Jews, and not just the Gentiles, were in bondage to "the basic principles of the world." We conclude, then, that "the basic principles" lie behind both paganism and Judaism outside of Christ.

Therefore, in spite of the many differences between Judaism and paganism, both involve subjugation to the same "basic principles of the world." "World" here must be understood as the evil world that stands in hostility to God. F. F. Bruce draws the devastating conclusion, "The demonic forces of legalism, then, both Jewish and Gentile, can be called 'principalities and powers' or 'elemental spirits of the world.' "[1]

In conclusion, "the basic principles of this world" seem to be the evil spiritual beings that lie behind both worldly philosophies and legalistic ethical systems, behind paganism and unsaved Judaism alike. Therefore, Paul's description of a believer as "no longer a slave, but a son" (Gal. 4:7) means that before God shed his grace upon us, we were in bondage to demons, who poisoned our mental and moral lives. God's antidote to their poison is Christ's mighty redemption that delivers us from slavery and makes us sons and daughters of God (Gal. 4:5).

Slavery Today?

Just in case you regard talk of slavery as ancient history, let's go back to fifth grade. Consider the true story of fifth graders from Aurora, Colorado. The students in Barbara Vogel's class had just finished studying the history of slavery in America when they discovered a newspaper article. It said that trade in human lives was still going on in Sudan, Africa's largest and poorest country. The slave trade has prospered as a weapon used by the fairer skinned Muslim rulers against the 4 million black, mostly Christian people living in southern Sudan. The Muslims had declared a *jihad*, a holy war of forced Islamization, against the Christians. Local militias fighting without pay for the Sudanese government claim booty in human lives. They have been quick to abduct the Christians' children for economic and sexual exploitation. What was the fifth graders' response to this news? Listen to their teacher's words:

"They sat at my seat, tears coming down their faces, that this evil had not been taken care of," Vogel said of her pupils.

"The first thing they said was, 'What are we going to do about this?' "

Then somebody piped up, "Haven't we learned from our past?"

The students started collecting change in jars to buy the freedom of one or two slaves. Then the word spread via newspapers and radio, and checks began pouring in. One year later, they had sent more than $50,000 to Christian Solidarity International to buy the freedom of slaves. Barbara Vogel's announcement on January 22, 1999, that 1,050 Sudanese had been purchased and set free was met by her students' cheers and tears of joy.[2]

Children of God and Children of the Devil

We can conceive of slavery today because it still exists in our world. But even if it didn't, we would still accept the Bible's teaching concerning our situation before the Father adopted us. And other biblical passages support our conclusion that people need to be adopted because of their slavery to sin and Satan. The apostle John divides humanity into two groups, the children of God and the children of the devil:

> He who does what is sinful is of the devil, because the devil has been sinning from the beginning. The reason the Son of God appeared was to destroy the devil's work. No one who is born of God will continue to sin, because God's seed remains in him; he cannot go on sinning, because he has been born of God. This is how we know who the children of God are and who the children of the devil are: Anyone who does not do what is right is not a child of God; nor is anyone who does not love his brother. (1 John 3:8–10)

Before our adoption into God's family, we belonged to another father, the devil. This doesn't mean that all unsaved persons are Satanists. In fact, many of them do not even believe that Satan exists! Instead, it means that, like the Jewish leaders who rejected Christ (John 8), we did the bidding of our cruel father, the devil. It means that, before we entered God's family, we walked in darkness under the sway of the Prince of Darkness.

Our conclusions concerning our need for adoption are confirmed by passages that speak of the devil's identity, activities, and goals. He is "the great dragon . . . that ancient serpent called the devil, or Satan, who leads the whole world astray" and deceives the nations (Rev. 12:9; 20:7). He is "the god of this age," who "has blinded the minds of unbelievers, so that they cannot see the light of the gospel of the glory of Christ, who is the image of God" (2 Cor. 4:4).

The sum of the matter is that our need for adoption is far greater than we might have imagined. Were we simply orphans? No, we were far more desperate than orphans. We were slaves of Satan and sin, but then the Son of God redeemed us, the Spirit of sonship opened our hearts, and the Father made us his own.

Thus far, this chapter has described the horrible situation before our adoption. Should we end on such a sour note? Certainly not. Although the person and work of Christ will be the focus of later chapters, this one would be sorely lacking without an effort to extol the unique Son of God, our Redeemer, Jesus Christ.

Our Hero

Before we contemplate Christ, let me tell you the true story of a train conductor who won an award for heroism for saving the life of a toddler:

Transportation Secretary Rodney Slater praised Norfolk Southern Railroad conductor Robert Mohr for "unselfishly risking his life to save the life of another person." He presented Mohr with the Transportation Department's Award for Heroism. Mohr and Rodney Lindley, a locomotive engineer who received a certificate of commendation, were operating a 96-car freight train on a run from Decatur, Illinois, to Peru, Indiana. While in Lafayette, Indiana, they spotted what turned out to be a 19-month-old girl, Emily Marshall. She had wandered away from her mother and onto tracks not far from her home. Mohr went down to the plow of the still-moving train to push Emily out of harm's way.[3]

Four things stand out in this story: Mr. Mohr's qualifications, Emily's plight, Mr. Mohr's action, and the wonderful results for the little girl. Mohr no doubt had a railroad conductor's license; he knew what he was doing. Emily's plight was obvious. Had Mohr not acted when he did, she would have been killed. Mohr's action is praiseworthy. He put himself in danger to rescue Emily. The results for Emily and her family, especially her mother, were marvelous.

One great passage of Scripture that connects bondage, redemption, and adoption is Galatians 4:3–7:

We were in slavery under the basic principles of the world. But when the time had fully come, God sent his Son, born of a woman, born under law, to redeem those under law, that we might receive the full rights of sons. Because you are sons, God sent the Spirit of his Son into our hearts, the Spirit who calls out, *"Abba,*

Father." So you are no longer a slave, but a son; and since you are a son, God has made you also an heir.

Now let's compare the four points we observed in the story of the heroic train conductor: his qualifications, the child's plight, the hero's action, and the wonderful results.

(1) *The hero's qualifications:* Jesus Christ was perfectly qualified to be our Redeemer. He, the eternal Son of God, came from heaven, became a human being, and was born of the Virgin Mary. In becoming incarnate, he came under the obligation to keep the law of God, and he did this perfectly.

(2) *Our plight:* we were slaves of the Evil One and under the curse of the law, with no possibility of rescuing ourselves.

(3) *The hero's action:* "Christ redeemed us from the curse of the law by becoming a curse for us" (Gal. 3:13). That is, he delivered us by bearing the law's penalty on behalf of us lawbreakers, when he died on the cross in our place.

(4) *The wonderful results for us:* we are no longer under the curse. Instead, we receive the blessing that God promised our father Abraham, when he said that he would bless all nations through him (Gen. 12:3). In a word, Christ took our curse and earned for us the blessings of sonship and an inheritance of eternal life.

Robert Mohr deserves credit for rescuing little Emily from death. The Lord Jesus Christ deserves eternal praise for redeeming us from sin and Satan. Listen to the choir in Revelation 5:9, 12:

You are worthy to take the scroll and to open its seals, because you were slain, and with your blood you purchased men for God from every tribe and language and people and nation. . . . Worthy is the Lamb, who was slain, to receive power and wealth and wisdom and strength and honor and glory and praise!

How do you suppose Emily's mother responded when she met her daughter's deliverer? What are the responses of believing hearts to the wonders rehearsed in Revelation 5? They are the same as those of the living creatures and the twenty-four elders: "The four living creatures said, 'Amen,' and the elders fell down and worshiped" (Rev. 5:14).

Crack Babies

More than likely, none of us will meet any slaves in our lifetime. Slavery is beyond our personal experience. If we really wanted to, however, we could meet crack babies. As a result of being born to mothers addicted to crack cocaine, these babies are born in bondage to crack. Their plight saddens us, but crack babies exist in our culture. Let me share with you a true account that illustrates the main point of this chapter. A friend named Chrishon tells his story:

Coming from an extended family that has adopted many children, the biblical concept of adoption is very warming for me. My relatives who adopted kids did so simply because they desired to. And they did so of their own free choosing; they were not obligated to do so. . . . What is so awesome is that, according to Scripture, before I was even born, God had chosen to adopt me. That is so comforting to me because it means no matter how bad I mess up, God loves me despite myself. And that's what adoption really is—genuine love. I know because I see it in my relatives. In human terms, it is only genuine love that can lead parents to adopt babies born addicted to crack. Human reason can't explain that. . . . My relatives could have chosen a "perfect" child to adopt and been all right. But they chose perhaps the hardest kids to adopt. They had to fight agencies that didn't like white families adopting black kids (not to mention the social persecution they faced) and doctors who told them to put the babies in institutions because they couldn't be controlled and would never be productive. But my relatives displayed true love, sacrificing sleep, money, time, etc., all to love their adopted child.

God did even more. We all are like crack babies: born helpless, in circumstances beyond our control. There is nothing redeeming about us. But God's genuine love led him to sacrifice his Son, so that we might be made his sons and daughters.

I cannot improve on Chrishon's illustration. I can, however, turn our attention to two songs that help us express our praise for such a great redemption.

Where Shall My Wond'ring Soul Begin?

Where shall my wond'ring soul begin?
How shall I all to heav'n aspire?
A slave redeemed from death and sin,
A brand plucked from eternal fire,

How shall I equal triumphs raise
Or sing my great Deliv'rer's praise?

O how shall I the goodness tell,
Father, which Thou to me hast showed?
That I, a child of wrath and hell,
I should be called a child of God;
Should know, should feel my sins forgiv'n,
And taste today the joys of heav'n![4]

'Tis Not That I Did Choose Thee

'Tis not that I did choose thee,
    for, Lord, that could not be;
This heart would still refuse thee,
    hadst thou not chosen me.
Thou from the sin that stained me
    hast cleansed and set me free;
Of old thou hast ordained me,
    that I should live to thee.

'Twas sov'reign mercy called me
    and taught my op'ning mind;
The world had else enthralled me,
    to heav'nly glories blind.
My heart owns none before thee,
    for thy rich grace I thirst;
This knowing, if I love thee,
    thou must have loved me first.[5]

4

Loved by the Father

O ne of the most moving testimonies of salvation that I have ever heard is that of Robert A. Petterson (not I, but a friend of mine), who, after fruitful pastorates in Tulsa and Houston, serves in an evangelistic ministry to media in New York City. Bob was conceived by an unmarried woman. He and his siblings were shuttled from one foster home to another, where their lives were a nightmare. They were physically abused in one home, and sexually abused in the next. Bob remembers eating from a dish on the floor like an animal. He has no good explanation as to why he was adopted and not his siblings. He laments when he thinks about their lives. One has been married seven times, another has been to prison twice, and on it goes.

For some reason, Mr. and Mrs. Petterson, who were unable to have children themselves, chose Bob's picture out of a book of children available for adoption. That is how Bob came to be included in their family. And now, many years later, Bob is not only a happily married man with a loving family, a successful pastor loved by his people, and a visiting professor at a seminary, but also an heir to a considerable estate! It turns out that the man who adopted him was a millionaire.

Why Are We the Children of God?

Bob Petterson's story is one of the best illustrations I know of the biblical truth of adoption. We, who once were, by fallen human nature, slaves to sin, even children of the devil, are now children of God! Can we do a better job than Bob of figuring out the reason for our adoption? Why are we the children of God? There are at least three good answers to these questions. We are God's children:

- because we believe the gospel (Gal. 3:26; John 1:12)
- because Christ died to redeem us (Gal. 4:5)
- because God chose us (Eph. 1:5) and loved us (1 John 3:1)

Note the plurality of correct answers. Notice also the varying degrees of ultimacy in the answers. The most immediate answer is that we are adopted through faith in Christ. More ultimate than our faith is Christ's redeeming work. Indeed, Christ's redemption establishes our faith and makes us Christians. The most ultimate answer to the question of why we are adopted is God's mysterious election. This happened before the creation of the world (Eph. 1:4; 2 Tim. 1:9).

The more ultimate answers do not make less ultimate answers illegitimate. God's election does not nullify Christ's death and resurrection. Instead, Christ came to put God's plan into action (2 Tim. 1:10). And Christ's saving work does not nullify our faith. Rather, it establishes it. It is not any faith that saves, but faith in the Lord Jesus Christ. Neither does election nullify our faith. Instead, it guarantees it. Let us investigate the ultimate source of our sonship.

The Source of Adoption—God's Gracious Election: Ephesians 1:3-14

"In love he [God the Father] predestined us to be adopted as his sons through Jesus Christ." That is the testimony of Ephesians 1:4–5. Let's place that passage in its literary context. If we were assigned the task of dividing Ephesians 1:3–14 into paragraphs, two clues would help us greatly. One is the occurrence of the phrase "to the praise of his glorious grace" in verse 6 and its echoes in verse 12, "for the praise of his glory," and verse 14, "to the praise of his glory." If we use these structural indicators to help us outline the passage, we come up with these three paragraphs:

- Ephesians 1:3–6
- Ephesians 1:7–12
- Ephesians 1:13–14

There is another clue to the division of Ephesians 1:3–14—topical analysis. If we carefully study the section, we find that it has a Trinitarian framework. It begins with praise directed to "the God and Father of our Lord Jesus Christ" (v. 3). Although Christ is mentioned throughout verses 3–14, the only mention of his saving work occurs in verse 7, "In him we have redemption through his blood." The Holy Spirit appears only once in verses 3–14, and that is in verse 13, where he is called "the promised Holy Spirit." Combining the references to the persons of the Trinity with the above divisions, we get three paragraphs:

- Ephesians 1:3–6: God the Father
- Ephesians 1:7–12: God the Son
- Ephesians 1:13–14: God the Holy Spirit

We should add one more piece of information to our outline. Each paragraph emphasizes a work that corresponds to the person of the Godhead named. Paragraph one speaks of God the Father's work of election. Paragraph two mentions God the Son's redeeming work. Paragraph three speaks of the Spirit as the seal (a mark of ownership and protection) that the Father puts on believers for the day of redemption. Here is how the chart looks when completed.

- Ephesians 1:3–6: God the Father's election
- Ephesians 1:7–12: God the Son's redemption
- Ephesians 1:13–14: God the Holy Spirit as seal

We must take into account Paul's purpose in writing this chapter of Ephesians. He begins with praise: "Praise be to the God and Father of our Lord Jesus Christ" (v. 3). And he ends the same way: ". . . to the praise of his glory" (v. 14). In between, he extols God's "glorious grace" and "glory" (vv. 6, 12). Clearly, the purpose of Paul's teaching is to elicit praise from the people of God for the grace of the Father, the Son, and the Holy Spirit.

After directing praise to God the Father for "every spiritual blessing in Christ" (v. 3), Paul mentions two particular blessings: sanctification and adoption (vv. 4–5). It is noteworthy that Paul's references to sanctification and adoption are preceded by references to the sovereign grace of God in salvation. God the Father "chose us in him before the creation of the world to be holy and blameless in his sight. In love he predestined us to be adopted as his sons" (vv. 4–5).

OUR SONSHIP: OUR FATHER
We are ready to look in more detail at the blessing of sonship in Ephesians 1:4–5. Every phrase is noteworthy. In

love *the Father* predestined us unto sonship. God is the Holy Trinity. He has eternally existed as three in one. He is one God, and we dare not separate the persons of the Godhead from one another. Yet Scripture does teach us to distinguish the Father, the Son, and the Holy Spirit, as we have observed in Ephesians 1:3–14, where the Father chooses, the Son redeems, and the Spirit is God's seal. Our adoption was initiated by God the Father, not by us. It is his part to select us to be members of his family. He did so even before he created the world. Such thoughts are difficult for us to comprehend. God the Father almighty, maker of heaven and earth, loved us like that? Most definitely. That is why Paul specifies that *in love* the Father predestined us to be his sons and daughters.

I have known few people with as positive a view of their father as Robyn:

> My earthly father has been instrumental in my life— to instruct me, discipline me, love me. He is the one person in the world that I trust the most. He has taken care of me. He has given me good things that I have not expected or deserved. His goodness to me humbles me. He is the one I always go to for advice and counsel because I highly respect him, know he is wise, and know that he loves me and wants the best for me. He will not advise me for his benefit. I do not fear manipulation because of his love for me. How much more is this true of my heavenly Father! "How great is the love the Father has given unto us that we should be called sons of God!" He loves me even more than my earthly father and with a perfect love, and with his omnipotence and with his omnis-

cience and with his omnipresence. He truly is a great and loving Father!

Most of us do not have as positive a father figure as Robyn does. Still, we who know Christ by God's grace have the same heavenly Father that she has. And he is great beyond measure. He is the Supreme Being in the universe. Unfortunately, in our zeal to emphasize the nearness and accessibility of God (biblical themes, to be sure), we have underestimated his greatness and majesty (equally biblical themes). As a result, we have lost a sense of wonder at the fact that this great God is ours. J. I. Packer puts matters in proper perspective:

> Today, vast stress is laid on the thought that God is *personal*, but this truth is so stated as to leave the impression that God is a person of the same sort as we are—weak, inadequate, ineffective, a little pathetic. But this is not the God of the Bible! Our personal life is a finite thing: it is limited in every direction, in space, in time, in knowledge, in power. But God is not so limited. He is eternal, infinite and almighty. He has us in his hands; we never have him in ours. Like us, he is personal; but unlike us, he is *great*. In all its constant stress on the reality of God's personal concern for his people, and on the gentleness, tenderness, sympathy, patience and yearning compassion that he shows toward them, the Bible never lets us lose sight of his majesty and his unlimited dominion over all his creatures.[1]

Packer suggests that we need to take more walks outside on starry nights and look up, for the heavens have much to teach us about God's greatness and our limitations.

Look at the stars. The most universally awesome experience that mankind knows is to stand alone on a clear night and look at the stars. Nothing gives a greater sense of remoteness and distance; nothing makes one feel more strongly one's own littleness and insignificance. And we who live in the space age can supplement this universal experience with our scientific knowledge of the actual factors involved—millions of stars in number, billions of light years in distance. Our minds reel; our imaginations cannot grasp it; when we try to conceive of unfathomable depths of outer space, we are left mentally numb and dizzy.

But what is this to God? "Lift up your eyes and look to the heavens: Who created all these? He who brings out the starry host one by one, and calls them each by name. Because of his great power and mighty strength, not one of them is missing" (Is 40:26). It is God who brings out the stars; it was God who first set them in space; he is their Maker and Master—they are all in his hands and subject to his will. Such are his power and his majesty. Behold your God![2]

Don't you see how contemplating God's character and works increases the wonder of adoption? This great God, by his grace, has made us members of his family. Surely here is abundant reason for us to worship God our Father. In fact, that is the primary reason he created us. The Creator made us to worship him, and in order that we might be grateful worshipers, he made us his sons and daughters. Seen in this light, how feeble is our worship! How inadequate is our praise! How selfish are our lives! Still, because he has adopted us by his grace, he will not put us out. He will love us forever. It is our place to bask in our Father's love and to love him in return. Above all people, the sons and daughters of the living God should know who he is and who they are, and consequently should live for his glory all the days of their lives.

OUR SONSHIP: SOVEREIGN GRACE

This brings us to two other important phrases in Ephesians 1:4–5: *in love* the Father *predestined* us to be his children. Predestination signifies God's choice of his people for salvation. The apostle insists that predestination is rooted in divine love. In this life, we will never understand every ramification of God's election of his people for salvation before the foundation of the world. But this much is plain: predestination is inseparable from God's love. Before time, the Father loved us and chose us to be members of his family. Jeff's vivid childhood memories help us to appreciate God's gracious choice:

> Studying adoption gives me fresh insight into my total lack of deserving anything good from God. It reminds me of grade school, when we would choose sides to play games. Often, I was picked toward the end because I wasn't good at sports. I have a vivid memory of once being one of the very first drafts. I still remember the feelings of being somewhere that I didn't deserve to be. In the case of the playground, it was ignorance on the chooser's part. With God, he knows full well whom he is choosing, yet he chose me anyway. This both humbles me and fills me with gratitude and joy.

Does our knowledge of God's gracious choice of us humble us and fill us with gratitude and joy? It should. It is not enough for us to be doctrinally sound. That is important, but it is not enough. We must also be warm to the Word of God, personally engaged with his truth. For us to say amen to the doctrines of grace and not be filled with gratitude to God for his grace shown to us means that we do not yet believe the doctrines of grace as God intended. Remember the purpose of election, according to Ephesians 1—that we might praise God for his glorious grace. If I cultivate doctrinal precision, but fail to allow God's truths to rule my heart, I am a Pharisee, a religious externalist. A proud Calvinist is an oxymoron, a contradiction in terms.

OUR SONSHIP: HELP FOR THE UNCONVINCED

Maybe you are still not convinced of the sovereignty of God's grace. If that is the case, we do not belittle you or speak down to you. Instead, speaking the truth in love, we want to show you the riches of God's grace. Listen to Ephesians 1:11–12: "In him we were also chosen, having been predestined according to the plan of him who works out everything in conformity with the purpose of his will, in order that we, who were the first to hope in Christ, might be for the praise of his glory."

I've heard dedicated Christians say that Ephesians 1 teaches the goal of election, but not its basis. They say that it tells us what God elected us unto, but not why he elected us; God left that a mystery. I do not deny that there is mystery involved in God's eternal election of his people. But verse 11 is not mysterious. It affirms in emphatic terms that the choosing was God's. Listen to the strong words again:

49

"In him we were also chosen, having been predestined according to the plan of him who works out everything in conformity with the purpose of his will." In plain words, Paul affirms that our election was due to God's sovereign choice of us.

Ephesians 1 does tell us the goal of election. But it also plainly and repeatedly tells us why God chose us—because of his love and will. Verse 4 says that he chose us before the creation of the world, so that we will understand that we had nothing to do with our salvation. We didn't even exist before the creation of the world.

But someone will respond, "God foresaw our faith and chose those whom he knew would believe in his Son. That's what 'he chose us in Christ' means." I reply, "Not so." Throughout Ephesians 1:3–14, the words "in Christ" and "in him" refer to union with Christ. God unites believers to his Son. He spiritually joins us to Christ, so that his benefits become ours. Verse 4 says, "He chose us in him [Christ] before the creation of the world." The words "in him" have the same meaning here as in the rest of the passage; they speak of union with Christ. The difference between verse 4 and the other references is that verse 4 speaks of God's decision before creation to unite us with Christ. That means that when God planned to save us, he also planned to join us to his Son in salvation. God not only chose a people for himself, but also planned the means by which to save them. He planned to send his Son to die and rise and to send the Spirit to bind his people to the Son in salvation.

The remainder of Ephesians 1:4–5 reinforces the conclusions we have reached concerning the freedom of God's grace in salvation. "In love he predestined us to be adopted as his sons through Jesus Christ, *in accordance with his pleasure and will.*" Ultimately, our adoption is according to the Father's good pleasure and will. It is his will that has the first and last word in salvation, not ours. Note in passing that he chose us to be adopted "through Jesus Christ." Our adoption is through the Son of God. Christ, the eternal Son, is the mediator of the Father's adoption. The grand theme of Christ's sonship in relation to ours will occupy us in the next two chapters. Now it is enough to repeat: the source of our adoption is God's gracious election.

Jennifer helps us meditate on the connection between God's sovereign love and our sonship:

> As we looked at adoption, what really struck me is God's love for me. My husband and I are currently in an adoption process trying to adopt a baby. It has so far been a long wait. I often think that God has forgotten me and our desire for a child. I was reminded that as desperately as I desire a child, God's love for me is even greater than that desire. I desire to lavish my love on a baby; God is lavishing his love on me.

Jennifer is in good company. The poets join her in trying to express the inexpressible—adequate praise for the sovereign grace of God:

> The love of God is greater far
> Than tongue or pen can ever tell;
> It goes beyond the highest star,
> And reaches to the lowest hell;
> The guilty pair, bowed down with care,
> God gave his Son to win;
> His erring child He reconciled,
> And pardoned from his sin.

Could we with ink the ocean fill,
And were the skies of parchment made,
Were every stalk on earth a quill,
And every man a scribe by trade,
To write the love of God above
Would drain the ocean dry.
Nor could the scroll contain the whole,
Though stretched from sky to sky.

[Refrain]
O love of God, how rich and pure!
How measureless and strong!
It shall for evermore endure
The saints' and angels' song.[3]

The Source of Adoption—God's Love: 1 John 3:1

The apostle Paul is the primary teacher of adoption in the New Testament, but he is not the only one. The apostle John also teaches about sonship in John 1:12 and 1 John 3:1–3.[4] This latter passage pertains to our topic at hand. Another way of saying that the source of our adoption is God's gracious election is to say that the source of our adoption is God's love. The passage deserves quotation:

> How great is the love the Father has lavished on us, that we should be called children of God! And that is what we are! The reason the world does not know us is that it did not know him. Dear friends, now we are the children of God, and what we will be has not yet been made known. But we know that when he appears, we shall be like him, for we shall see him as

he is. Everyone who has this hope in him purifies himself, just as he is pure.

To "be called children of God" by God the Father is to be adopted by him (1 John 3:1). Here, too, adoption is based on the Father's great love for us. The ultimate reason for our sonship is God's electing love. I have not read a better human description of this love than that of Darlene, an adoptive parent:

> My thoughts on adoption do take on a personal element as my son Lorenzo is adopted. Putting myself in his place as an infant, I see him alone and without a family of his own, and I remember how my heart jumped when I first saw him at five months old. If my frail human heart could expand like that, I stand in awe of a God who loved me so much to want to include me in his family.

That's it, exactly. The Father loved us so much that he chose to include us in his family. As a result, what can we do except love him and keep his commandments? First John 3:3 has it right: "Everyone who has this hope in him purifies himself, just as he is pure." Here is the highest motivation for the Christian life: we love him because he first loved us. We work hard and do his will out of gratitude for grace received, even grace received in adoption. As the sons and daughters of God the Father, we continually magnify his grace in worship, witness, work, and play. His fatherhood and our sonship determine our very existence. Here is a biblical description of who we are: "In love he [the Father] predestined us to be adopted as his sons" (Eph. 1:4–5). We are the sons and daughters of the living God. May our Father write this truth deep in our hearts, help us to believe it, and enable us increasingly to live, not as orphans, but as we are in truth, the children of our heavenly Father.

I pray that we, along with Maura Ellen, would be overwhelmed with God's sovereign grace and kneel in thanksgiving:

> The truth of God the Father's adoption of me causes me to be overwhelmed with his love. The fact that the Father would choose me as a part of his family is beyond my comprehension. My earthly family has no choice. I am a part of them; they must accept the good and bad in me simply because I was born into their family. God, however, who knows *all* the good and bad in me, has chosen me to be a part of his family and has offered me the great riches that are his. Simply the thought of adoption overwhelms me and brings me to my knees in thanksgiving.

The Son of God, Our Brother

*I*t is easy to be moved by the pitiful story of a nine-year-old boy who lived with his mother's corpse for a month, rather than give her up. When thirty-year-old Crystal Wells, a single mother, died on November 3, 1999, in Memphis, her son Travis put her coat over her body and covered her face with notebook paper. Travis continued to go to school every day and fixed his own meals, mainly cereal and frozen pizza. A month after Crystal's death, neighbor Dorothy Jeffries came to the Wellses' apartment and found Crystal's body. Dorothy told how Travis had begged her not to call the police because he was afraid that he would have to go to a foster home.

"When the ambulance came, he ran to his mother because he didn't want her to be taken. I will never forget that sight," she said. "It was the saddest thing I have ever seen in my life."[1]

Travis had one person in the world, his mother. His actions after her death were futile attempts to preserve the bond between them. Thankfully, however, there is a bond that is stronger than death. That is why Revelation 14:13

records, "Blessed are the dead who die in the Lord from now on." How could the dead be truly happy? Because they died "in the Lord," that is, in union with the Lord Jesus Christ. Everyone who is spiritually joined to Christ enjoys eternal life now, will experience greater bliss at death, and will know the greatest joy in the resurrection.

How do sinful human beings become united to the Son of God with an unbreakable bond? What does union with Christ have to do with adoption? In this chapter, we will attempt to answer these questions and more as we consider:

> *The incarnation of the Son*
> *The adoption of the Son*
> *Our union with the Son*

The Incarnation of the Son

THE SON'S ETERNITY

Christians sometimes give the impression that Christ's sonship began with his birth in Bethlehem. To be sure, he was born as a human being in Bethlehem. But his life as the Son of God had no beginning. Accordingly, the place for us to begin discussing the sonship of the Son of God is before the creation of the world. Jesus makes it plain in his famous prayer in John 17 that God's fatherhood and Jesus' sonship did not begin at the Incarnation: "Father, I want those you have given me to be with me where I am, and to see my glory, the glory you have given me because you loved me before the creation of the world" (v. 24). Here Jesus prays that believers may join him and the Father in heavenly glory. In so doing, he states that the Father loved him before creation. That means that there never was a time when the

Father was not a Father and the Son was not a Son. The Father's fatherhood and the Son's sonship are eternal. This reveals one of the Son's qualifications for making us children of God. He is the divine Son of God.

THE SON'S INCARNATION

Although the Son of God has always been the Son, fallen human beings are not automatically God's children. In order for us to become his children, a connection had to be made between God and us. That connection was made by the Son's incarnation. The eternal Son of God became a human being, as Paul states in Galatians 4:4–5: "God sent his Son, born of a woman, born under law, to redeem those under law, that we might receive the full rights of sons." The Father sent his Son into the world to be born of the Virgin Mary, so that he could grow up to be our Redeemer.

The eternal Son of God became "flesh" (John 1:14), a man of flesh and blood, apart from sin. The writer to the Hebrews explains, "Since the children have flesh and blood, he too shared in their humanity so that by his death he might destroy him who holds the power of death—that is, the devil—and free those who all their lives were held in slavery by their fear of death" (2:14–15). The Son of God shared in our humanity, becoming a human being like us, in order to defeat the Evil One and redeem us from bondage.

God the Son became a human being, and in so doing established a connection between God and man. His humanity created a fraternity, a bond with human beings. This bond was essential if we were to be saved. But it did not automatically save us. Instead, it was divine preparation for the Son to perform mighty deeds that resulted in the salvation of his people.

HIS SONSHIP AND OURS

Christ's sonship is unique in some ways, and in other ways it is like ours. He showed the uniqueness of his sonship by healing a lame man on the Sabbath. The Jewish leaders were unsettled. "For this reason the Jews tried all the harder to kill him; not only was he breaking the Sabbath, but he was even calling God his own Father, making himself equal with God" (John 5:18). They misinterpreted the Old Testament Sabbath regulations and were scandalized when Jesus miraculously enabled a lame man to walk on the Sabbath day.

But Jesus presented an even greater stumbling block to them, when he claimed for himself a divine sonship that far exceeded any with which they were familiar. The Jewish leaders considered themselves sons of God by virtue of their belonging to the nation of Israel. Nonetheless, they were shocked when Jesus said, "My Father is always at his work to this very day, and I, too, am working" (John 5:17), because Jesus was putting his healing work on a par with the mighty acts of God. By calling God his Father, Jesus was claiming equality with God, the ability to do works that only God can do. For a mere mortal to make such a claim is to blaspheme, but for the unique Son of God to make that claim is to tell the truth.

If Jesus' sonship is unique, does that mean that his sonship is unlike ours in every way? No, it doesn't. In fact, by virtue of Jesus' incomparable sonship, all believers in him become sons of God. We who know the Son have the same Father as he does, as Jesus told Mary Magdalene on the first Easter Sunday: "Go . . . to my brothers and tell them, 'I am returning to my Father and your Father, to my God and your God' " (John 20:17). God the Father is Jesus' Father—

and ours, too, if we know Jesus as Lord and Savior. As a result, we belong to the same family as Jesus, the family of God. Jesus, therefore, refers to his disciples as "brothers." Indeed, because Jesus and we are "of the same family," he "is not ashamed to call" us "brothers" (Heb. 2:11). The Son of God is a Brother like no other.

Lisa's mother died when she was five, and God has used her brother Shannon to help her ever since. She tells her story:

> Christ is our elder brother. I have a brother who is eleven years older than me. Throughout my life, Shannon has been there for me. Often in a crisis he will call to make sure I am okay and offer some advice. Because of the age difference, Shannon often has insight into different areas of life, including issues with my parents. He also is my protector. As a perfect older brother, Jesus uses his wisdom to guide and protect me. He looks out for my best interests. He is always there for me in times of crisis. There is no older brother like him.

The Adoption of the Son

The Son's incarnation was essential preparation for our union with him and our adoption that flows from it. He who always existed as God the Son became a human being to make us God's children. Because Jesus is the unique Son of God, he is perfectly qualified to do the work needed for us to be spiritually joined to him and adopted by the Father. What is that work? We will address that question as we consider the Son's adoption.

In the second psalm, God says concerning King David,

59

"You are my son; today I have become your Father" (Ps. 2:7). The king of Israel was God's son in a special sense. In addition, every worthy occupant of David's throne prefigured the coronation of the great Son of David who was to come, Jesus Christ. For this reason, the New Testament applies Psalm 2:7 to Jesus a number of times. Let's investigate them.

JESUS' BAPTISM

At Jesus' baptism (Matt. 3:17), God the Father proclaims Jesus' adoption as incarnate Son. After the Spirit descends on Jesus like a dove, the Father speaks from heaven: "This is my Son, whom I love; with him I am well pleased." The Father's words, "This is my Son," allude to Psalm 2:7 and are fulfilled in Jesus' coronation as King in his resurrection and return to the Father. Do these words contradict the conclusion we reached earlier that Jesus' sonship is eternal? No, here the Father speaks of his adoption of the eternal Son as his incarnate Son. He who always was the Son by virtue of his deity is adopted as God's Son by virtue of his humanity. The Father uses Jesus' baptism as an occasion to proclaim his sonship. At the same time, the Father makes known his delight with his Son and the work he came to do. By submitting to baptism, the sinless Christ consecrates himself to God and identifies with those he came to save—sinners in need of divine cleansing.

JESUS' TRANSFIGURATION

At Jesus' transfiguration, the Father again announces the adoption of his Son. Six days after predicting his death and resurrection, Jesus takes along Peter, James, and John and ascends a mountain (Matt. 17:1). There the apostles see Jesus' "majesty" (2 Peter 1:16), for "his face shone like the sun, and his clothes became as white as the light" (Matt. 17:2). Moses and Elijah appear, and Peter blunders by suggesting, in an attempt to prolong the experience, that he build three shelters, one each for Jesus and the Old Testament figures.

The Father points to the risen Christ's adoption as the God-man when he utters words identical to those at Jesus' baptism, "This is my Son, whom I love; with him I am well pleased" (v. 5). He who for all eternity was the divine Son of God in heaven has become the divine-human Son of God on earth. There is a hint of his saving work at the Transfiguration, when the chief topic of conversation between Moses, Elijah, and Jesus was Jesus' "departure, which he was about to bring to fulfillment at Jerusalem," that is, his redemptive death and return to the Father (Luke 9:31).

JESUS' RESURRECTION

Specifically, in Jesus' resurrection, the Father mightily proclaims the adoption of his incarnate Son. On his first missionary journey, at Antioch in Pisidia, Paul contrasts two radically different estimations of Jesus—that of the Jewish leaders and that of God. The Jewish leaders reject Jesus and condemn him to death; by contrast, the Father highly esteems his Son and publicly announces his righteousness by raising him from the dead (Acts 13:27–30).

The apostles are witnesses to the risen Savior. Paul explains that Jesus' resurrection is a fulfillment of Scripture: "We tell you the good news: What God promised our fathers he has fulfilled for us, their children, by raising up Jesus. As it is written in the second Psalm: 'You are my Son; today I have become your Father'" (Acts 13:32–33, quoting

Ps. 2:7). By raising Jesus from the dead, the Father adopts his eternal Son as mediator.

Paul begins his epistle to the Romans on a similar note. The gospel concerns God's "Son, who as to his human nature was a descendant of David, and who through the Spirit of holiness was declared with power to be the Son of God by his resurrection from the dead" (Rom. 1:3–4). The point deserves repetition: Christ does not begin to be God's Son when he is raised from the dead; rather, the resurrection powerfully declares his incarnate sonship. This is the redemptive deed that the unique Son accomplishes to make us children of God—he dies for sinners and is raised by the Father in public proclamation of his adoption.

JESUS' ASCENSION AND SESSION

The Father broadcasts Jesus' adoption at his ascension. Using Psalm 2:7, the writer to the Hebrews links the Father's proclamation of the God-man's sonship with his sitting down at God's right hand:

> After he had provided purification for sins, he sat down at the right hand of the Majesty in heaven. So he became as much superior to the angels as the name he inherited is superior to theirs. For to which of the angels did God ever say, "You are my Son; today I have become your Father"? (Heb. 1:3–5)

After making atonement for sins by his death on the cross, Jesus is raised from the dead, ascends into heaven, and sits at the Father's right hand. Theologians call this sitting with God Jesus' session. Jesus' heavenly session demonstrates his superiority over the angels, because no angel occupies that place of honor and authority. Only the victorious Son of God sits there.

Moreover, Hebrews teaches, Jesus' name "Son" also lifts him above the angels. God has never adopted an angel as his son, but the Father adopted the risen and ascended Lord Jesus as his Son when he rose, ascended, and sat down at the Father's right hand in heaven. At the Son's session, the Father declared the words of Psalm 2:7, "You are my Son; today I have become your Father" (Heb. 1:5).

CONCLUSION

Unlike sinners, the Son of God was never a child of the devil needing redemption from sin. Rather, he is the Father's eternal and sinless Son. Still, when the Father sends the Son into the world to redeem sinners, he adopts Jesus as his incarnate Son. At Jesus' baptism and transfiguration, the Father testifies that Jesus is his beloved Son (Matt. 3:17; 17:5). Specifically, the apostles apply Psalm 2:7 ("You are my Son; today I have become your Father") to Jesus' resurrection and ascension/session (Acts 13:32; Heb. 1:5). The Father adopts his incarnate Son by raising him and seating him at his own right hand as King.

How do these truths help us understand *our* adoption? By God's grace, Jesus' adoption becomes ours. After making atonement, the Son of God was adopted in his resurrection and return to the Father. By virtue of our union with the Son, the Father places us *in Christ* as adult sons and daughters in his family. Let's further explore union with Christ.

Our Union with the Son

The eternal Son became a man and was adopted by his Father as his divine-human Son in his resurrection/ascension. The Son's adoption is the basis for our union with him and our adoption. Yet, we are not actually adopted into God's family until we are joined to Christ. Who unites us to Christ and his benefits, including adoption?

THE WORK OF THE HOLY SPIRIT

Although the Holy Spirit performs many ministries for believers, his main one is to join us to Christ. Paul teaches that truth when he talks about the church as the body of Christ: "For we were all baptized by one Spirit into one body—whether Jews or Greeks, slave or free—and we were all given the one Spirit to drink" (1 Cor. 12:12–13). Although Christians differ in many ways from one another, including ethnic background ("Jews or Greeks") and social situation ("slave or free"), they are all incorporated into the church by the Holy Spirit. We all "drink," or partake of, the Spirit when we trust Christ as our saving substitute.

Paul teaches that possession of the Spirit is essential to being a Christian: "If anyone does not have the Spirit of Christ, he does not belong to Christ" (Rom. 8:9). The Spirit's joining people to the Son of God is so vital that if someone lacks the Spirit, he or she lacks Christ.

Paul explains the biblical background of union with Christ in two passages in Ephesians. The unsaved are "separated from the life of God" (Eph. 4:18). Indeed, they are "separate from Christ, . . . without hope and without God in the world" (Eph. 2:12). People need union with the Son because they are separated from God and salvation. The good news is that "now in Christ Jesus you who once were far away have been brought near through the blood of Christ" (v. 13).

Paul expresses union with Christ in two main ways. First, scores of times he uses the prepositional phrases "in

Christ" or "in him." Thus, the verse just quoted means, "Now *in union with Christ Jesus* you who once were far away have been brought near" (v. 13). And when Paul expresses his heartfelt desire to "gain Christ and be found in him," he means to "be found *in union with Christ*" and all that that entails, including justification, of which Paul immediately speaks (Phil. 3:8–9).

Second, Paul affixes a preposition meaning "with" to verbs that describe Christ's redemptive deeds. He can say, therefore, that believers "died with Christ" (Col. 2:20), were "raised with Christ" (Col. 3:1), ascended "with Christ" (Col. 3:3), were seated "with him in the heavenly realms" (Eph. 2:6), and even "will appear with him in glory" (Col. 3:4). The apostle teaches that when we are spiritually joined to Christ, all of his saving accomplishments become ours.

UNION WITH THE SON OF GOD

Union with the Son brings to us all the benefits of salvation. Paul writes: "Praise be to the God and Father of our Lord Jesus Christ, who has blessed us in the heavenly realms with every spiritual blessing in Christ" (Eph. 1:3). The Father has adorned his people with all spiritual blessings in union with his Son. This fact is confirmed if we view the blessings separately. (In each passage I have italicized the words that indicate union with Christ.)

(1) *Regeneration:* "God, who is rich in mercy, made us alive *with Christ* even when we were dead in transgressions" (Eph. 2:4–5).

(2) *Justification:* "God made him who had no sin to be sin for us, so that *in him* we might become the righteousness of God" (2 Cor. 5:21).

65

(3) *Sanctification:* "You are *in Christ Jesus,* who has become for us wisdom from God—that is, our . . . holiness and redemption" (1 Cor. 1:30).

(4) *Preservation:* "I am convinced that neither death nor life, neither angels nor demons, neither the present nor the future, . . . nor anything else in all creation, will be able to separate us from the love of God that is *in Christ Jesus our Lord*" (Rom. 8:38–39).

(5) *Glorification:* "When Christ, who is your life, appears, then you also will appear *with him* in glory" (Col. 3:4).

Clearly, each aspect of salvation comes to us in union with God's beloved Son. That includes adoption.

UNION WITH THE SON AND OUR ADOPTION

Union with the Son brings adoption with it. That is taught in at least two New Testament passages. First, Galatians 3:26–27 says, "You are all sons of God through faith in Christ Jesus, for all of you who were baptized into Christ have clothed yourselves with Christ." Paul explains that when the Galatians were baptized, they were joined to Christ. Baptism "into Christ" means baptism into a relationship with him. Furthermore, Paul likens baptism to changing clothes. As a suit of clothes covers the body, so "being clothed with Christ" means being covered with him, being united to him.

Paul does not mean that everyone who is baptized is automatically saved. Rather, he means that baptism signifies union with the Son. And, since verses 26 and 27 are connected by the word "for," Paul intends for his readers to understand that union with Christ is the cause of adoption:

"You are all sons of God through faith in Christ Jesus, *for* all of you . . . have clothed yourselves with Christ." The word "for" indicates that the Galatians are adopted through faith because they were baptized into union with Christ.

Second, Romans 8:17 also links adoption to union with Christ: "Now if we are children, then we are heirs—heirs of God and co-heirs with Christ, if indeed we share in his sufferings in order that we may also share in his glory." Paul teaches that God's adopted children can look forward to an inheritance. Then Paul attaches a condition: we will inherit if we share in Christ's sufferings. Paul means that the children of God are identifiable. They are in union with Christ in his death and resurrection, and that union manifests itself as believers suffer with him now. That union will also manifest itself in the future, as believers share in his glory. Here Paul regards union with the crucified and risen Son as undergirding the adoption of God's genuine sons and daughters.

Conclusion

John Calvin understood these truths well:

> As long as Christ remains outside of us, and we are separated from him, all that he has suffered and done for the salvation of the human race remains useless and of no value for us. Therefore, to share with us what he has received from the Father, he had to become ours and to dwell within us. For this reason, he is called "our Head" [Eph. 4:15], and "the first-born among many brethren" [Rom. 8:29]. We also, in turn, are said to be "engrafted into him" [Rom. 11:17], and to "put on Christ" [Gal. 3:17]; for, as I have said, all that he possesses is nothing to us

until we grow into one body with him. It is true that we obtain this by faith. Yet since we see that not all indiscriminately embrace that communion with Christ that is offered through the gospel, reason itself teaches us to climb higher and to examine into the secret energy of the Spirit, by which we come to enjoy Christ and all his benefits.[2]

The Son of God became a human being to join us to himself in salvation. The Father declared his sonship at his baptism and transfiguration. When he raised the Son from the dead and seated him at his right hand in heaven, the Father adopted him by declaring, "You are my Son; today I have become your Father" (Ps. 2:7). The eternal Son's adoption as the incarnate Son becomes ours when the Holy Spirit joins us to Christ. All of the blessings of salvation, including adoption, are ours when the Spirit unites us to Christ, the Son of God and our Brother.

Redeemed by the Son

There is a true and tragic story of a Baptist minister who rescued his son. David Johnson Sr., 45, a Primitive Baptist pastor, was fishing with his seven-year-old son, David Johnson Jr., from the bank of Percy Priest Lake near Smyrna, Tennessee. Young David slipped on the bank and fell into the lake. His father jumped into the water and managed to push his son toward a rock, and the boy climbed out. But Pastor Johnson could not swim. Before his son could return with two fishermen whom he summoned from the road, the elder David had disappeared. Later his body was found about twenty-five feet from shore in sixteen feet of water.

The story pulls our emotions in opposite directions. We rejoice at the father's heroism in risking his life to deliver his son. But we are saddened at the terrible cost of the deliverance. And the knowledge that Pastor Johnson left behind a wife and two other children besides David adds to our grief.

There is a much greater deliverance than the one just recounted. It also involves a son, but this time the son is the deliverer. When sensitive hearers first learn about this deliverance, they experience conflicting emotions, too. But this time they are saddened at the plight of the son, and are overjoyed at what comes to those whom he rescues. Scripture speaks of these matters: "But when the time had fully come, God sent his Son, born of a woman, born under law, to redeem those under law, that we might receive the full rights of sons" (Gal. 4:4–5).

The saving work of the unique Son of God, expressed in terms of adoption, is a redemption. We customarily understand redemption as a synonym for salvation, and that is not wrong, because Scripture uses the word in that way. But we miss something unless we appreciate the first-century cultural background of redemption.

A document from A.D. 86, for example, records the liberation of a slave named Euphrosyne "under Zeus, Earth, Sun for a ransom."[1] This record contains the three key elements in the redemption of a slave: the state of bondage, the payment of a redemption price (a ransom), and the resultant state of freedom. Those three elements suggest three ways of profitably viewing Jesus' redemption of his people:

> *Our need for redemption*
> *The price of redemption*
> *The results of redemption*

Our Need for Redemption

Before God made us members of his family, we were slaves to sin, needing to be redeemed. Paul writes of Christ, "In him we have redemption through his blood, the forgiveness of sins, in accordance with the riches of God's grace that he lavished on us with all wisdom and understanding" (Eph. 1:7–8). In another place, the apostle exalts the Father, who "has rescued us from the dominion of darkness and brought us into the kingdom of the Son he loves, in whom we have redemption, the forgiveness of sins" (Col. 1:13–14). Plainly, the Bible points to redemption as bringing about the forgiveness of our sins. The implication is that our sinful condition constituted our need for redemption. We were enmeshed in evil and could not free ourselves. Listen to what Titus 2:13–14 says: "Jesus Christ . . . gave himself for us to redeem us from all wickedness and to purify for himself a people that are his very own, eager to do what is good."

The Price of Redemption

This brings us to the redemption price. God claimed all the firstborn Israelite males when he passed over the homes of the Israelites who had put blood on their doorframes before their exodus from Egypt (Ex. 12:12–13; 13:2). Later, he substituted the Levites for the firstborn males (Num. 3:40–51). But the number of the firstborn was greater than the number of Levites. Consequently, God commanded that a redemption price of five shekels per man be paid "to redeem the 273 firstborn Israelites who exceed the number of the Levites" (Num. 3:46–47). As a result, 1,365 shekels of silver were paid to Israel's priests (Num. 3:50–51).

Peter contrasts this redemption of the Jewish firstborn with a far greater redemption price than the slaughtered animals of the Exodus or the shekels that ransomed the firstborn: "For you know that it was not with perishable things such as silver or gold that you were redeemed from the empty way of life handed down to you from your forefathers, but with the precious blood of Christ, a lamb without blemish or defect" (1 Peter 1:18–19). The great redemption price was the blood, the violent death, of the Son of God.

The Bible commonly speaks of that as a voluntary self-giving on Christ's part: "For even the Son of Man did not come to be served, but to serve, and to give his life as a ransom for many" (Mark 10:45). "Christ Jesus . . . gave himself as a ransom for all men" (1 Tim. 2:5–6). "Our great God and Savior, Jesus Christ . . . gave himself for us to redeem us" (Titus 2:13–14). Jesus freely gave his life as a ransom in place of the prisoners of sin. He gave himself to set free all who would believe in him. He willingly died to redeem his people from their sins. Our response should be to willingly offer ourselves to him in worship and service.

Galatians 4:4–5 ties together the Redeemer's person and work: "But when the time had fully come, God sent his Son, born of a woman, born under law, to redeem those under law, that we might receive the full rights of sons." In the fullness of redemptive history, God the Father sent his unique Son into the world to be born of the Virgin Mary. Why? His Son became a human being in order to redeem sinners. Christ was not only born of Mary, but also under obligation to obey the holy law of God. And obey it he did, perfectly, his whole life. Moreover, he "became obedient to death—even death on a cross!" (Phil. 2:8).

An earlier passage in Galatians vividly portrays the Redeemer's great redemption in connection with the law. After dealing with our failure to keep God's law, Paul states,

> All who rely on observing the law are under a curse, for it is written: "Cursed is everyone who does not continue to do everything written in the Book of the Law." Clearly no one is justified before God by the law, because, "The righteous will live by faith." The law is not based on faith; on the contrary, "The man who does these things will live by them." (Gal. 3:10–12)

Paul opposes the Judaizers who insisted that fidelity to Jewish ways is required for admission into the people of God. Not so, says the apostle. No one can keep the law so as to merit God's favor. No one is good enough. As a result, the curse of the law hangs threateningly over the head of every lawbreaker. The thunderbolt of the curse of the law is ready to strike each of us with what we deserve—the wrath of a holy and just God.

Just when he brings his readers to the brink of despair, Paul tells of God's gracious solution to their insuperable problem: "Christ redeemed us from the curse of the law by becoming a curse for us, for it is written, 'Cursed is everyone who is hung on a tree' " (Gal. 3:13). Here, in graphic terms, Paul tells of the cost of our redemption. The cost is nothing for us who believe in the Son of God, who loved us and gave himself for us. God saves us freely by his grace. Paul's whole point in the verses leading up to Galatians 3:13 is that we are helpless to deliver ourselves.

Consequently, we need a deliverer, one who can do for us what we cannot do for ourselves. His name is the Lord Jesus Christ. Although redemption for us is all of grace and therefore costs us nothing, for him the price was steep. Redemption cost the Son of God everything. In God's plan, Jesus became so closely associated with the penalty that we lawbreakers deserved, that Paul says he became a curse for us. He died on a cross, a death that was accursed, as stated by Deuteronomy 21:23, which Paul quotes as "Cursed is everyone who is hung on a tree."

But didn't thousands of people die by crucifixion under Roman rule? Wasn't the road to Rome lined with crucified slaves who took part in the rebellion of Sparticus? The answer to both questions is yes. Well, then, what makes Jesus' crucifixion different? How can his sufferings help others? The answer to these questions lies in the identity of the Redeemer that we discussed in the last chapter. Because he is the God-man, the incarnate Son of God, he is able to rescue others. His was no ordinary crucifixion; his was the death of the Son of God. As a result, Jesus redeemed us from the curse of the law by suffering the curse, the penalty, in our place. The thunderbolt of the curse of the law that should have struck our sinful heads struck his holy one instead. Our Redeemer set us free.

Ever since Christ's great ransom, Christians have sung songs praising him for his mighty redemption. Fittingly, we will do so for all eternity, as Revelation 5 reminds us when it lauds the Lamb of God:

> You are worthy to take the scroll and to open its seals, because you were slain, and with your blood you purchased [redeemed] men for God from every tribe and language and people and nation. You have made them to be a kingdom and priests to serve our God, and they will reign on the earth. (Rev. 5:9–10)

The Results of Redemption

"God sent his Son, born of a woman, born under law, to redeem those under law, that we might receive the full rights of sons" (Gal. 4:4–5). We are ready now to take a look at two of "the full rights of sons."

1. *Redemption sets us free.* When the Redeemer redeems us, he sets us free! This fact completes the adoption metaphor. When we were slaves to sin, Christ redeemed us with his blood. Consequently, we are the free sons and daughters of

the living God. "You did not receive a spirit that makes you a slave again to fear, but you received the Spirit of sonship" (Rom. 8:15).

Some unsaved people gain a tremendous sense of liberation when they come to Christ. This is especially true of those who come from a cultic background. For thirty years, William J. Schnell served the Watchtower Society as a faithful Jehovah's Witness. Later, as a Christian, he wrote a book entitled *Thirty Years as a Watchtower Slave*. His story of redemption is worth retelling:

> Then one night, I could stand it no longer. I was home alone that night, my wife being away on a visit to her parents. I sank to my knees. I threw myself unreservedly upon the Lord. All night long I poured out a confession of all the wrongs I had done as a Watchtower slave. . . . I poured out an account of all my sins, iniquities and failures before the Lord that night. But I also thanked the Lord that in spite of it all He had not forsaken me. I thanked Him for preservation and for all the wonderful things that He had done for me while I was thus doing these wrongs.
>
> Finally, early in the morning, I promised the Lord and vowed to Him that I would write an exposé and publish all these facts if He would liberate me . . . [from] my fear of Jehovah's Witnesses and the dire things they threatened to do to me.
>
> Now as early dawn broke in the East, I arose from my knees. God had heard my prayers. I stood up by the grace of God a free man! I stood up calm, assured, with peace in my mind and heart. I stood up

knowing I should never be afflicted by fear of the
Watchtower Society, and Jehovah's Witnesses and
what they could do to me. . . . God had forgiven me,
and for the first time in thirty years I actually experienced a peace which goes beyond human understanding. . . . I had emerged from the labyrinth of
the Watchtower slavery into "the glorious liberty of
the children of God" (Rom. 8:21).

We are prone to forget the stupendous fact that there is
great freedom in the Lord Jesus Christ! And that freedom
belongs not only to those who come to Christ from backgrounds of bondage. Sometimes Christians also need to experience a greater measure of the freedom that Christ
purchased. As exhibit A, consider that Paul's admonition in
Galatians 5:1 wasn't written to unbelievers, but to believers:
"It is for freedom that Christ has set us free. Stand firm,
then, and do not let yourselves be burdened again by a yoke
of slavery."

Lisa is a recent example of a believer who has been set
free:

Adoption is attractive to me because it is the perfect
antidote to legalism. I never understood how caught
up in legalism I was. It was such a subtle but driving
force in my life. I kept trying to be good enough for
God, but despaired at how impossible the task was.
At the very heart I was afraid of one thing: at some
point I would do something terrible and consequently lose my salvation. Although the church I
was raised in preached assurance of salvation, I often
wondered if I believed it mostly because I wanted it

to be true. The confusion came from the fact that although the churches I attended said they believed in the assurance of salvation, they preached a list of things one had to do to be a "good Christian." I got the feeling that if you failed in any of those areas, you probably were not saved to begin with.

The study of adoption has clarified the confusion I once felt. Adoption is a legal procedure which secures a child's identity in a new family. The adoptive parents take the child into family court on a specific day, documents are signed, and from that point on the child belongs in the family.

As a teacher's assistant, I often work with children in the foster system. These children still legally belong to one of their parents, or the state of Missouri, but they live with another family. Because of the transient nature of a foster home, many kids feel very insecure. They are allowed to stay with their foster family only if they perform correctly.

God didn't choose to be our foster parent. We don't get kicked out of the family because of our behavior. We don't have to worry day to day whether or not we are good enough to be part of the family. In his infinite kindness, God made us a permanent part of his family. We can focus our energy, not on performing well, but on enjoying family life. Studying adoption has helped me see that when I accepted Christ as my Redeemer, I became a permanent member of his family. Nothing can undo the legal procedure that binds me to Christ. He died to redeem me. He signed the adoption papers, so to speak, with his blood. Nothing can cancel the work he did for me. I am free from the fear of falling away. Hallelujah!

2. *We belong to our Father.* A second benefit of sonship is ownership. Paradoxically, at the same time that Christ's redemption liberates us, he claims us as God's own. This is taught in 1 Corinthians 6:18–20:

> Flee from sexual immorality. All other sins a man commits are outside his body, but he who sins sexually sins against his own body. Do you not know that your body is a temple of the Holy Spirit, who is in you, whom you have received from God? You are not your own; you were bought at a price. Therefore honor God with your body.

Paul speaks specifically of sexual sin, but in so doing he sets forth a principle that applies to many other areas of life, too: Redemption results in God's ownership of the redeemed. We were purchased at a tremendous price: the blood of Christ. As a result, we belong to God the Father. We are his and must live for him the rest of our lives. John Stott captures this truth well:

> Bought by Christ, we have no business to become the slaves of anybody or anything else. Once we were the slaves of sin; now we are the slaves of Christ, and his service is the true freedom.[2]

That last sentence encapsulates the blessed paradox of the Christian life. "Once we were the slaves of sin; now we are the slaves of Christ, and his service is the true freedom."

How foolish we were before we trusted the Redeemer! Although we were in bondage to sin and even Satan, we considered ourselves most free. We viewed Christianity as bondage. How God has changed our view of things! Now we know that previously we were miserable slaves and that in Christ we have been set free. Our liberation is not only release from the clutches of evil. It is also embrace by the strong arms of our God and Father. And—write it on the doorposts of your mind—the reason we are free is that the Redeemer accomplished a mighty redemption on our behalf. As a result, we are liberated from sin to love and serve God our Father.

What Difference Does It Make?

It is our Father's will that these truths make a difference in our lives. First, Christ redeemed us that we might become the worshiping children of God. The chief purpose for which we exist is to worship our Father. May our children see such a zeal for the worship of God in us that they will find the Christian faith irresistible.

Second, Paul's warning, "It is for freedom that Christ has set us free. Stand firm, then, and do not let yourselves be burdened again by a yoke of slavery" (Gal. 5:1), is for each of us. Let us humbly appropriate the grace of God in the power of the Spirit and always be vigilant lest we get snared by the deceitfulness of sin. And if you find yourself snared, even now, then reach out for help. Don't continue in bondage another day! Cry out for help to a trusted brother or sister in Christ. Your salvation doesn't begin the day you die and go to be with Christ. It has begun now. Christ is a mighty Redeemer. Glorify him by living in the victory that he purchased.

Third, the Son of God redeemed us so that we might reach out to others with the liberating message of adoption. A Christian who doesn't witness is like a fish that doesn't swim—it's a contradiction in terms. Jesus is a wonderful Redeemer, and sonship was meant to be shared.

Fourth, it is for good reason that the apostle Paul enunciates the principle of redemption resulting in ownership in the context of sexual immorality in 1 Corinthians 6. Men are the same in the twenty-first century as they were in the first. They are easily seduced by sexual temptation. And our day has forms of sexual temptation that the apostle Paul never dreamed of. In a church of one hundred people, there have to be men who are burdened with guilt because of their involvement with pornography via the Internet, magazines, television, etc. It is pervasive. The temptations are too strong, and we are too weak. We need the help of other brothers, who will hold us accountable for what we allow our eyes to see. He is not a wimp who realizes his weakness and reaches out for help. Rather, he is a wise man. Reach out today.

We have meditated on the great redemption that the Redeemer, Jesus Christ, provided for us. May God grant us grace that we might live in a manner worthy of the high calling we have received. May our families see us as the free sons and daughters of the living God. May unsaved neighbors, fellow workers, and friends be attracted to the Son of God because of the beauty of Christian freedom that is evident in our lives. But wait; all of this is beyond us. We are weak and the task is impossible. Where does our confidence reside for any victory in these areas? As contemporary Christian singer Don Francisco insists in his song "I'll Never Let Go of Your Hand," it does not reside in us, but in our mighty Father:

I know what you've been hearing;
   I've seen you hide your fear,
Embarrassed by your weaknesses,
   afraid to let Me near.
I wish you knew how much I longed
   for you to understand,
No matter what may happen, child,
   I'll never let go of your hand.

[Chorus]
The life that I have given you
   no one can take away
'Cause I've sealed it with my Spirit, Blood and Word.
The everlasting Father
   has made His covenant with you,
And He's stronger than the world you've seen and heard.[3]

7

Drawn by the
Spirit of Sonship

*R*ecently the town hall's computer in Echallens, Switzerland, was programmed to identify the local children who were ready to start kindergarten. The computer read only the last two digits of each citizen's age. As a result, a 105-year-old gentleman, a retired school teacher no less, received a notice to attend elementary school along with sixty-five five-year-olds. The computer program has since been corrected. Prospects are bright that all other 105-year-olds in the town will be spared such an embarrassment.[1]

Whether we are five, 105, or somewhere in between, we become children of God in the same way. How we enter God's family can be viewed in two ways—from the perspectives of human responsibility and divine sovereignty. We become children of God:

> *By faith in Christ*
> *By the work of the Holy Spirit*

Faith in Christ

We become sons and daughters of God the Father by believing in Christ. Faith in Christ is the means of our adoption. This is plainly taught in Galatians 3:26–29:

> You are all sons of God through faith in Christ Jesus,
> for all of you who were baptized into Christ have
> clothed yourselves with Christ. There is neither Jew
> nor Greek, slave nor free, male nor female, for you
> are all one in Christ Jesus. If you belong to Christ,
> then you are Abraham's seed, and heirs according to
> the promise.

The Galatians became children of God "through faith in
Christ Jesus." The Father places us in his family as adult sons
and daughters when we trust Christ as offered in the gospel.
In this respect, adoption is parallel to justification, God's gracious declaration that sinners are righteous and their sins are
forgiven. Justification, like adoption, is through faith, as Paul
underscores in Galatians 2:15–16:

> We . . . know that a man is not justified by observ-
> ing the law, but by faith in Jesus Christ. So we, too,
> have put our faith in Christ Jesus that we may be
> justified by faith in Christ and not by observing the
> law, because by observing the law no one will be
> justified.

In this brief passage, Paul three times speaks of being
justified by faith in Christ and three times denies that people are justified by observing the law.

In Galatians 3:6–9, Paul teaches that people become
children of Abraham by being justified through faith:

> Consider Abraham: "He believed God, and it was
> credited to him as righteousness." Understand, then,
> that those who believe are children of Abraham.

The Scripture foresaw that God would justify the Gentiles by faith, and announced the gospel in advance to Abraham: "All nations will be blessed through you." So those who have faith are blessed along with Abraham, the man of faith.

In the last verses of the same chapter, Paul teaches a complementary truth: "You are all sons of God through faith in Christ Jesus," and "if you belong to Christ, then you are Abraham's seed, and heirs according to the promise" (Gal. 3:26, 29). We become sons of Abraham through justification (Gal. 3:6–7) and adoption (Gal. 3:26, 29). And both are by faith.

Does this mean that justification and adoption are exactly the same? No, it means that they overlap. Sinners are both adopted and justified by God's grace through faith in God's Son. In addition, justification and adoption are both legal metaphors. But justification occurs in the criminal division of the court, while adoption takes place in the family court. Of his free grace, God the Judge declares righteous (justifies) condemned sinners when they trust Jesus as Lord and Savior. Of his free grace, God the Father places in his family (adopts) all slaves of sin who trust his unique Son as their Redeemer.

John also mentions adoption. After noting that many to whom Jesus came rejected him, John writes: "Yet to all who received him, to those who believed in his name, he gave the right to become children of God" (John 1:12). To grant the right to become children of God is equivalent to adoption. Notice who receive adoption—"those who believed in his name." John agrees with Paul, then, that sonship is received by faith.

Barbara Curtis describes the day the bottom dropped out of her world:

> I remember the day my dad left. He knelt and hugged me and cried. The skimpy dress of a five-year-old girl could not protect me from the chill that gathered around my arms and legs. The scratchy tickly whiskers—would I feel them no more? The arms that felt so safe—would they be gone forever?

For more than thirty years, Barbara struggled to find herself—and, eventually, God. It was not an easy journey. She endured foster homes, living with relatives, growing up to believe in herself, substituting success in academia for a father's love, only to feel more lonely than ever—and, finally, trying the New Age movement. All of this left her empty. In God's good time, however, he drew her to himself, as she explains:

> How ready I was the moment I first understood that God was my Father. At last, I was someone's little girl! To this day, ten years later, I cannot approach God intellectually, but only as a child and with no reservations, I feel such love: "Though my father and mother forsake me, the Lord will receive me" (Ps. 27:10).

Barbara says that the extent of her loss prepared her to drink deeply from the fountain of God's love. And she came to know the Father's love the only way anyone does—by faith:

> I remember once, before he left, my father carrying me home in his arms as blood gushed from a jagged

cut on my foot. I was four and I was frightened, hoping that my father could take care of me. But though that day he stopped the bleeding, no earthly father could have healed the wounded heart he later left behind. That hurt cried out for the love of a heavenly Father. And so I will always be God's grateful little girl—trusting, dependent, and filled with faith in the arms that will never let me go.[2]

Adoption is by grace through faith. That is true, but if isolated from other aspects of God's truth, it can be misleading. We have looked at the means of adoption only from the human side. Is God at work when we believe in Christ and receive sonship? The answer is yes, as we shall now see.

The Work of the Holy Spirit

We become sons and daughters of God by the work of God the Holy Spirit. It is easy for us to think of God the Father and God the Son having parts to play in our adoption. Their names are so appropriate to communicate God's grace of sonship. God is *the Father* who places us as adult children in his family. God is *the Son* who redeems us with his blood, so that we belong to the Father's family. But the name *Holy Spirit* is not familial, as are *Father* and *Son.* So what does God do to impress upon our hearts the depth of his fatherly love for us? He alters the name of the third person of the Trinity! He is called "the Spirit of his Son" (Gal. 4:6) and "the Spirit of sonship" (Rom. 8:15).

Let's examine the Spirit's role in adoption, according to Galatians 4:6 and Romans 8:15–16. In the former text we learn, "Because you are sons, God sent the Spirit of his Son into our hearts, the Spirit who calls out, 'Abba, Father.' " By sending the Spirit of his Son into the hearts of his sons and daughters, the Father confirms their adoption. God really makes us his children and gives us the Spirit as a pledge of this fact. What a pledge—God himself! The Spirit, given to us, calls out, "Abba, Father." This means that the Spirit not only assures us, but also enables us to address God as Father.

These truths are confirmed in Romans 8:15–16, where we learn about two ministries of the Spirit of adoption. First, "the Spirit himself testifies with our spirit that we are God's children" (v. 16). This is the inner witness of the Spirit. The Holy Spirit personally, supernaturally, individually, and inscrutably assures us of our sonship. It is as if the Spirit of God whispers deep within our hearts, "I love you. You are mine. I am Father to you, and you are my beloved child."

Second, it is "by" the Spirit that "we cry, 'Abba, Father' " (v. 15). This means that the Spirit enables us to address God sincerely as "Father." The faith that we exercise in becoming God's sons and daughters is a gift of God. Many of us were unaware that the Spirit of God was drawing us when we came to faith in Christ. All we knew was that we were trusting Christ as Lord and Savior. And indeed we were. But God's grace was working even then. The Spirit of sonship was working in our hearts, and it was by his grace that we called out in faith to God the Father for salvation. In fact, if the Spirit had not enabled us to call God "Father," we never would have done so.

Conclusion

There are, therefore, two good answers to the question, "How do we become sons of God?" We are adopted by faith, and the Spirit enables us to believe. In sum, the means of adoption is Spirit-enabled faith in Christ.

TWO APPLICATIONS
Let me suggest two applications of these truths.

Adoption gives us a fresh way to present the gospel. The ways in which God applies salvation to us can be thought of as tools in a toolbox. In the toolbox are many tools: justification, sanctification, regeneration, calling, conversion, and perseverance. Nevertheless, at times we have hammered with a pair of pliers and tried to saw with a screwdriver. We can do better. We need to become familiar with all of the God-given tools for evangelism and edification. For too long we have overlooked a handy tool that has been lying at the bottom of the box—adoption. It is useful for both evangelism and discipleship. Let's think now about the first of those.

Here is an outline for presenting the gospel in terms of sonship:

(1) *Our need:* we are in bondage to sin (Gal. 4:3, 7).
(2) *God's provision:* the Father sent his Son to redeem us with his blood (Gal. 4:4–5; 3:13).
(3) *Our response:* we become God's children by trusting Christ as Savior (Gal. 3:26; John 1:12).

This may prove to be an effective way of witnessing to people who suffer from a sense of alienation, as so many do today. Perhaps there is someone reading this who does not know the Son of God as Redeemer. For you I have three things to say. First, you, like the rest of us, are a sinner in bondage to your sins (Gal. 4:3, 7). One who is stronger than you has you in his clutches, and you cannot free yourself. You need a mighty Redeemer to rescue you.

Second, the good news of the Bible is that God the Father sent just such a Redeemer. He is Jesus Christ, the eternal Son of God. The Father sent him to be born of the Virgin Mary, so he could become a human being just like us, except for sin. He was born under obligation to keep God's law. This he did perfectly for his whole life. Finally, he laid down his life by dying on the cross in our place. "Christ redeemed us from the curse of the law by becoming a curse for us" (Gal. 3:13). This means that he suffered the penalty we lawbreakers deserve. He died the accursed death we should have died—and all because he loved us.

Third, I hope that you are asking, "What must I do to be rescued?" You must despair of making any effort to save yourself. Cast yourself entirely on the mercy of Jesus Christ. If you believe that he died and rose again to redeem you, then you are redeemed. You become a child of God by trusting the Son of God to deliver you. This is the gospel in terms of sonship. We appeal to you: trust the Son of God today as your Redeemer from sin. He is trustworthy to save all who come to the Father through him.

I rejoice at the power of God's Word. In 1998, I spoke at a men's retreat sponsored by Chapelgate Presbyterian Church in Marriottsville, Maryland, where Ron Steel is the pastor. I delivered simple messages on adoption and watched God work. The men in the meetings were visibly moved by the healing biblical words of sonship. In small groups they told of God's working in their lives to heal old wounds, to restore relationships, and to bring them to repentance.

And God saved the best till last. As we were driving out of the conference center, we noticed a man sitting on a large rock with his head in his hands. The driver of our car stopped to inquire as to the man's welfare. "Thank you," he replied. "I'm fine. My brother is down the hill being led to the Lord by Pastor Steel." Ron Steel told me later that he had presented the gospel to the man in terms of sonship. The message of adoption became to that man a cool drink on a sticky day. It ministered refreshment to his thirsty soul. In addition, he was immediately convicted about his lack of love for his wife, which had resulted in the near destruction of their marriage.

We must trust the Holy Spirit for results in evangelism. This second application flows from the fact that the means of adoption is Spirit-enabled faith in Christ. We are unable to cause people to believe. All of our good arguments and sincere love cannot make a child of God out of a child of the devil. Only the Spirit of sonship can do that. We are dependent upon the Spirit to convert unbelievers. Ron Steel knew where the credit belonged for the salvation of the man whom he led to Christ at the retreat in Maryland:

> I have seen ripe fruit before, the kind where you just give a little tug and it comes off the tree in your hand. I have seen fruit that fell off the tree when you put your hand underneath it. But I don't remember fruit quite so ripe as this fellow. It was as if I had to duck because the fruit came flying off of the tree in my direction. The Lord used the messages on adoption to bring the man to himself. His conversion was entirely the work of the Holy Spirit. I merely witnessed the man's profession out loud of what God had already done in his heart. To God belongs all the glory.

Pastor Steel has it right. To God belongs all the glory because God, specifically the Holy Spirit, effectively draws people into the Father's family. Does this mean that we don't need to share our faith? Should we repeat the famous words, "Sit down, young man. When God is ready to save the heathen, he will do it without your help or mine," as a hyper-Calvinistic pastor told William Carey in an attempt to discourage the young shoemaker from setting sail for India as a missionary? Not at all. Thank God that William Carey rejected the hyper-Calvinistic counsel of his elders and went to India anyway. He became a key figure in modern missions.

BUT WHY EVANGELIZE?

The question remains: Why should we evangelize, if only the Holy Spirit can convert sinners? There is a similar question: Why should we witness, if God chooses certain people for salvation? These are good questions that deserve thoughtful answers. Here are four:

God commands us to share our faith. We should bear witness of Christ in obedience to God's Great Commission, even if we don't have any better answer to these thorny questions. We are responsible to obey God's commands, not only when we can figure out his ways, but also when we remain in the dark. Understanding is not always a prerequisite for obedience. It is the task of God's servants to obey, whether or not they understand their Master's mind.

We don't know whom God will save. We are ignorant of many things that God knows. One of those things is the identity of the elect. God knows those whom he has chosen, but we don't. We can recognize the elect only when God draws them to salvation in response to the gospel. This is taught in 1 Thessalonians 1:4–5: "For we know, brothers loved by God, that he has chosen you, because our gospel came to you not simply with words, but also with power, with the Holy Spirit and with deep conviction." Because we are ignorant of the identity of the elect, we freely share the gospel with all, trusting God to bring his people to himself.

God sovereignly uses means. We not only evangelize *despite* God's absolute sovereignty in all aspects of salvation. We witness *because* God is absolutely sovereign in all aspects of salvation. It is a simple fact of Scripture and experience that God uses means to accomplish his ordained ends. If you were to ask a Christian woman where she places her ultimate confidence for her continued good health, she would say, "In God." If you then inquired as to why, if her ultimate confidence for her well-being was in God, she ate and slept every day, exercised regularly, didn't drink poison, and so forth, she would probably look at you as if you were crazy. The point is, we do not regard God's sovereign protection of us as incompatible with our exercising human responsibility to take care of ourselves. We live as if it were reasonable to avail ourselves of God's ordained means (our eating, sleeping, etc.), knowing that he has sovereign control of the end (his taking care of us). It *is* reasonable, as another example will show.

If you ask a Christian man where he places his ultimate trust for the well-being of his family, he will not say, "In my job security, disability plan, and pension program." Instead, he will say, "In God." If, on the other hand, this Christian were to conclude that, because God owns the cattle on a thousand hills, he could quit his job and trust God to slaughter a few of those cows, you would not commend him for his faith. And you would be in good company, for the apostle Paul gave this rule: "If a man will not work, he shall not eat" (2 Thess. 3:10). Here again, we regard God's ordained means (expecting us to work for a living) as compatible with his sovereignty over all things (even our financial security).

It is the same in evangelism. God is supreme. God the Father sovereignly chooses people for adoption before the creation of the world (Eph. 1:5). God the Son sovereignly redeems them in the Cross (Gal. 4:5; 3:13). God the Holy Spirit sovereignly enables people to call God "Father" (Rom. 8:15). *We* do not choose people for salvation, die on the cross, or open hearts to the gospel. Nevertheless, God has commanded us to witness, and if we are faithful, we will obey his command. And as we do, we are employing God's ordained means to his ends. He has planned to use the means of person-to-person evangelism to accomplish his end of bringing his people to salvation. That is why Paul writes,

> Remember Jesus Christ, raised from the dead, descended from David. This is my gospel, for which I am suffering even to the point of being chained like a criminal. But God's word is not chained. Therefore, I endure everything for the sake of the elect, that they too may obtain the salvation that is in Christ Jesus. (2 Tim. 2:8–10)

Notice that Paul believes that certain people are "the elect." Notice also that he doesn't for that reason take his ease. Rather, because of God's sovereign grace, Paul is driven to endure personal suffering, even imprisonment, so that the elect may hear the gospel, believe it, and be saved. Paul regards God's goal of choosing people for salvation, and his means of using witnesses of the gospel, as compatible; so should we. In fact, this leads to the fourth reason why we should witness, even though only the Spirit of sonship can make people into children of God.

God's sovereign grace guarantees results. Instead of stifling evangelism, belief in God's supremacy in salvation stimulates evangelism. We can be led by the Spirit to pray for, or witness to, people anywhere in the world, knowing that God's people are there. I recall being mildly amused, fifteen years ago, when I learned that a group of students at the school where I taught, Biblical Theological Seminary in Hatfield, Pennsylvania, were gathering to pray for the country of Albania. Why Albania? They deliberately chose the most difficult mission field in the world to magnify God's grace. At the time, Albania was an officially atheistic country, complete with a museum to atheism. I recall privately regarding the students as foolhardy at best and as spiritual show-offs at worst.

Well, it turned out that the joke was on me. God answered the students' prayers; with the demise of Communism in Europe, Albania was opened to Christian missions. At the museum of atheism, the gospel was preached. My students were more consistent in their application of the Reformed theology that I taught them than I was. God's sovereign grace transcends all boundaries, political or otherwise. And his grace guarantees results.

Let's ask God to use us to reach out to lost people under the Spirit's leadership. And let's trust the same Spirit who enabled us to call God "Father," to work in the lives of those to whom we share the Good News that they, too, may become a part of the family of God.

8

Adopted and Born Again?

*I*n his justly famous book *Knowing God*, J. I. Packer demonstrates how the knowledge of God is central to the Christian life:

> You sum up the whole of New Testament teaching in a single phrase, if you speak of it as a revelation of the Fatherhood of the holy Creator. In the same way, you sum up the whole of New Testament religion if you describe it as the knowledge of God as one's holy Father. If you want to judge how well a person understands Christianity, find out how much he makes of the thought of being God's child, and having God as his Father. If this is not the thought that prompts and controls his worship and prayers and his whole outlook on life, it means that he does not understand Christianity very well at all. For everything that Christ taught, everything that makes the New Testament new, and better than the Old, everything that is distinctively Christian as opposed to merely Jewish, is summed up in the knowledge of the Fatherhood of God. "Father" is the Christian name for God.[1]

Packer is right. Knowing the Father lies at the heart of the Christian faith. Scripture paints two different pictures to tell how we become God's children: adoption and regeneration. Adoption is the Father's placing believers in his family as adult sons and daughters. Regeneration is the Father's giving new life to sinners so that they become his children. In this chapter, we will consider the following aspects of regeneration:

> *The need for regeneration*
> *The Trinity and regeneration*
> *The fruit of regeneration*
> *Adoption and regeneration*

The Need for Regeneration

Ephesians 2:1–3 describes our need for regeneration:

> As for you, you were dead in your transgressions and sins, in which you used to live when you followed the ways of this world and of the ruler of the kingdom of the air, the spirit who is now at work in those who are disobedient. All of us also lived among them at one time, gratifying the cravings of our sinful nature and following its desires and thoughts. Like the rest, we were by nature objects of wrath.

This—one of the ugliest pictures in the Bible—depicts the plight of those outside of Christ. They are spiritually dead, living according to the dictates of the world system opposed to God, walking in the ways of the Evil One, and fulfilling their sinful desires, and so they are objects of God's wrath. The first and last of these descriptions concern us now.

Before God worked in our lives, we "were dead in" our "transgressions and sins" (Eph. 2:1). Paul means that unsaved people are devoid of the life of God. They are spiritually dead. They do not have eternal life and consequently do not know God. Jesus explains, "Now this is eternal life: that they may know you, the only true God, and Jesus Christ, whom you have sent" (John 17:3). Those who lack eternal life, therefore, do not have a personal relationship with God through Christ.

The unsaved are like the Allies' cryptographers in World War II before they broke the German code. They could see the letters on the page, but couldn't make sense of them. When the code was broken, the dead messages came alive and the Allies intercepted the plans of the Axis powers. Similarly, many testify to reading Scripture before they knew Christ. They could learn the stories and even memorize the words, but only after trusting Christ as their Savior did the Bible come alive to them. As Jesus said, "No one can see the kingdom of God unless he is born again" (John 3:3). One must first gain spiritual life (be born again) before one gains spiritual sight.

The last description of the lost in Ephesians 2:3 is also important: "We were by nature objects of wrath." A literal rendering is, "We were by nature *children* of wrath." Before God's regenerating grace came into our lives, we were "by nature," that is, by birth, "children of wrath." Paul here uses an Old Testament idiom. To "be a child of" something means "to deserve" that thing. For example, King David uses this expression to denounce the rich man (in Nathan's story) who took his poor neighbor's pet lamb. David said (literally), "The man who did this is a son of death" (2 Sam. 12:5). The NIV translates this as "The man who did this deserves to die!" Accordingly, when Paul calls us "children of wrath," he means that we deserve the wrath of God because of our sins.

Why does God paint such a dismal portrait of unsaved persons in Ephesians 2:1–3? Why does he teach that they are spiritually dead and deserving of his wrath? For the same reason that jewelers use a purple or black cloth as background for displaying precious stones. Diamonds shine brightest against the backdrop of the jeweler's cloth. Similarly, we only appreciate our salvation in light of the miserable state from which we were delivered. Ephesians 2:1–3 only begins a chapter. Listen to the very next words: "But because of his great love for us, God, who is rich in mercy, made us alive with Christ even when we were dead in transgressions—it is by grace you have been saved" (Eph. 2:4–5). The awfulness of our sin only serves to highlight the greatness of God's "love," the richness of his "mercy" and "grace." Notice how the Great Physician provides the very cure that fits our disease: when we were spiritually dead, he "made us alive with Christ." But, we might ask, what roles do the Father, Son, and Holy Spirit play in our regeneration?

The Trinity and Regeneration

Christians commonly think of the Holy Spirit when they speak of people being born again. That is not wrong, because the Spirit brings about regeneration. But it is a mistake to ignore the roles of the Father and the Son. The apostle Peter speaks of those roles:

> Praise be to the God and Father of our Lord Jesus Christ! In his great mercy he has given us new birth into a living hope through the resurrection of Jesus Christ from the dead, and into an inheritance that

can never perish, spoil or fade—kept in heaven for you, who through faith are shielded by God's power until the coming of the salvation that is ready to be revealed in the last time. (1 Peter 1:3–5)

Each member of the Trinity has a part to play in regeneration. The Father has mercifully "given us new birth"; that is, he has willed for us to be born again. Here is how James puts it: "He chose to give us birth through the word of truth" (James 1:18). The Father plans our regeneration. He is the mastermind, if you will, of the new birth.

The Son is also involved. The Father regenerates us "through the resurrection of Jesus Christ from the dead" (1 Peter 1:3). Jesus' resurrection is vital to our being born anew. If the Father is the planner of our regeneration, the Son is its source, because his resurrection makes us alive. We receive the new life of regeneration when the Father joins us to the Son. "God . . . made us alive with Christ" (Eph. 2:5).

Jesus sometimes speaks of regeneration as spiritual resurrection:

> Whoever hears my word and believes him who sent me has eternal life and will not be condemned; he has crossed over from death to life. I tell you the truth, a time is coming and has now come when the dead will hear the voice of the Son of God and those who hear will live. . . . Do not be amazed at this, for a time is coming when all who are in their graves will hear his voice and come out—those who have done good will rise to live, and those who have done evil will rise to be condemned. (John 5:24–25, 28–29)

Jesus contrasts "a time" that "is coming," namely, the future resurrection of the dead from their graves (vv. 28–29), with "a time" that "is coming and has now come" (v. 25). This latter time is that of Jesus' earthly ministry. Anyone who believes Jesus' message already has eternal life and "has crossed over from death to life" (v. 24). This crossing over is a spiritual resurrection in which the spiritually dead gain eternal life. Talking about regeneration as spiritual resurrection shows that it is a mighty act of God, as much as his raising the dead on the Last Day. It also points to the Spirit's role.

The Father plans regeneration and the Son in his resurrection supplies the power of the new life. What part does the Holy Spirit play? The Spirit applies regeneration to individuals. He makes them alive spiritually. Jesus teaches the necessity of the new birth: "No one can see the kingdom of God unless he is born again" (John 3:3). Jesus likens the Holy Spirit to the wind: "The wind blows wherever it pleases. You hear its sound, but you cannot tell where it comes from or where it is going. So it is with everyone born of the Spirit" (v. 8). Jesus here makes a play on words, by using the same words for "Spirit" and "wind." He wants his hearers to think of the Holy Spirit as the Wind of God. There are three similarities between the two.

First, Jesus says of the wind, "You hear its sound, but you cannot tell where it comes from or where it is going" (v. 8). He means that the wind is unpredictable—and so is the Spirit of God. Who can predict where and when the Spirit will work in hearts to convict people of sin and bring them to faith? The Spirit's work is incomprehensible. We see its results, but we can't predict beforehand or fully understand how and where the holy Wind of God blows.

Second, both the wind and the Spirit are sovereign. "The wind blows wherever it pleases" (John 3:8). Jesus here gives to the wind the human characteristic of volition. In so doing, he leads his hearers to think about the Spirit as choosing and willing. The Wind of God blows wherever he pleases! At times the Spirit surprises us by choosing to work in unlikely people or in unexpected ways. The wonderful thing is that he is pleased to work at all—and in people like us. We should more greatly reverence the Spirit and his work.

Third, the wind and the Spirit are only recognized by their effects. John doesn't spell this out for the wind; he lets us infer it. We can't see the wind; we see only the clothes swaying on the line or the leaves rustling on the trees. "So it is with everyone born of the Spirit" (John 3:8). We can't see the Spirit either, but we know that he has passed by this way because of the results he left behind. He causes people to be born again. He gives new life to people who were spiritually dead. It is no wonder that Paul speaks of "rebirth and renewal by the Holy Spirit" (Titus 3:5).

It is helpful to compare God to an electric company and eternal life to electricity. The Father is the C.E.O. of the company. He plans to supply the electricity of eternal life to our homes. The Son is the dynamo that produces the electricity that we depend upon so fully for (eternal) life. The Spirit is the worker who comes to our door and hooks up our home to the power supply, so we actually get electricity. Similarly, the Father plans regeneration, the Son's resurrection is the power supply, and the Spirit turns the juice on in our lives, actually giving us spiritual life.

It is both humbling and wonderful to consider that regeneration is the work of the Father, the Son, and the Holy

Spirit in our behalf. It took the Trinity to make us—dead sinners—alive to God, to cause us to be born again, to give us new life. Such thoughts humble us because they underscore how bad off we were before we tasted God's grace. As a result, we should be very thankful to the Trinity for loving us so much. Every believer in Christ is the object of the Father's mercy, enjoys the eternal life unleashed by the Son's resurrection, and knows God only because the Holy Spirit opened the door of his or her heart. It is no wonder, then, that Peter begins his teaching on regeneration by saying, "Praise be to the God and Father of our Lord Jesus Christ! In his great mercy he has given us new birth into a living hope through the resurrection of Jesus Christ from the dead" (1 Peter 1:3).

The Fruit of Regeneration

Our lives reveal our spiritual condition. John makes this point most emphatically: "This is how we know who the children of God are and who the children of the devil are: Anyone who does not do what is right is not a child of God; nor is anyone who does not love his brother" (1 John 3:10).

Let's study 1 John to examine the fruit that characterizes those born of God.

THE FRUIT OF CONFESSION OF SIN

The first fruit is surprising. At first glance, 1 John seems to teach perfectionism, the idea that Christians can attain a state of sinlessness before death. A prime example is 1 John 3:9: "No one who is born of God will continue to sin, because God's seed remains in him; he cannot go on sinning, because he has been born of God" (see also 5:18). This verse cannot teach perfectionism, because 1:8–10 emphatically denies the possibility of sinlessness in this life: "If we claim to be without sin, we deceive ourselves and the truth is not in us. . . . If we claim we have not sinned, we make him out to be a liar and his word has no place in our lives." And verse 9 states, "If we confess our sins, he is faithful and just and will forgive us our sins and purify us from all unrighteousness."

John is gracious to his readers. Before he exhorts them (in chapters 2–5) to excel in faith, love, and holiness, he reminds them (in chapter 1) that, even as Christians, they still sin. Therefore, they need to receive every day the forgiveness and cleansing that 1 John 1:9 promises to God's repentant children. If we detach the rest of 1 John from the first chapter, we will be dismayed. How many Christians exhibit complete faith in God, love their fellow believers perfectly, and live faultless lives? The answer is none. Because none of us is perfect, 1 John 1:9 is the perfect medicine for us. Each day we need the forgiveness and purification that God offers his children who come to him in repentance and faith. Let us take this medicine faithfully.

THE FRUIT OF FAITH IN THE SON OF GOD

It is the Father's will for his children to believe correctly concerning his beloved Son. Accordingly, 1 John urges us to believe in the Incarnation of the Son of God. Belief in the Incarnation is so important that John uses it to distinguish false spirits from the Holy Spirit:

> Dear friends, do not believe every spirit, but test the spirits to see whether they are from God, because many false prophets have gone out into the world. This is how you can recognize the Spirit of God:

Every spirit that acknowledges that Jesus Christ has
come in the flesh is from God, but every spirit that
does not acknowledge Jesus is not from God. This is
the spirit of the antichrist. (1 John 4:1–3)

The children of God also believe in Jesus' unique sonship: "The Father has sent his Son to be the Savior of the
world. If anyone acknowledges that Jesus is the Son of God,
God lives in him and he in God" (1 John 4:14–15; see also
5:5). In addition, they believe that Jesus is the Christ, the
Messiah promised in the Old Testament: "Everyone who believes that Jesus is the Christ is born of God" (5:1; see also
2:22–23).

A word of caution is in order. Robert Dunzweiler, a
beloved seminary professor of mine, shared with our class
his intense struggles as a new believer. He attended a Christian college and went faithfully to chapel. He was confused
as speakers presented the gospel in different terms. One said
that we must trust Christ as Savior, another that we must receive him by faith, another that we must repent, and still another that we must confess him as Lord.

Bob suffered greatly as he continually searched his soul.
"I trusted and received, but did I repent?" And later, "I believed, received, and repented, but did I confess Christ as
Lord?" How relieved he was to realize that the speakers
were saying the same thing in a variety of ways. Then, Bob
rested in Christ, in whom he had already believed, and
found assurance.

Similarly, it would be wrong to think that John intends
for us to take three different steps of faith—believing in the
Incarnation, Christ's sonship, and his messiahship. Rather, he
wants us to believe in the unique Son of God who became a

human being in fulfillment of Old Testament prophecy, loved us, and "laid down his life for us" (1 John 3:16). This truth is so important to him that he expresses it in various ways.

THE FRUIT OF LOVE FOR THE FATHER AND HIS CHILDREN

The children of God are filled to overflowing with the Father's love for them, and that love spills over in love for the Father and his children. John leaves no doubt that the source of this flow of love is God himself:

> God is love. This is how God showed his love among us: He sent his one and only Son into the world that we might live through him. This is love: not that we loved God, but that he loved us and sent his Son as an atoning sacrifice for our sins. (1 John 4:8–10)

God the Father, one of whose qualities is love, has deeply loved his children by giving his Son to die for them, so they would have eternal life. The new life that they have from God manifests itself in love for others: "We love because he first loved us" (1 John 4:19). They love their dear Father, who first loved them. Believers love the Father and love God (5:1–3).

A corollary of loving the Father is loving other Christians: "Whoever loves God must also love his brother" (1 John 4:21). John makes it plain that the love with which we love others is God's love for us: "Dear friends, let us love one another, for love comes from God. Everyone who loves has been born of God and knows God. Whoever does not love does not know God, because God is love" (4:7–8). Love for God and fellow believers, then, is a fruit of regeneration.

The Father's powerful love flowing through his children can heal wounded hearts, as Chardial explains:

> Prior to coming to know the love of God my Father, I felt completely and totally alone in life. My mother never showed affection or nurturing. I felt like an outcast due to my religion at that time; I was a member of Jehovah's Witnesses. I don't think I ever really had a sense of belonging. However, since I have trusted Christ as Savior, I have a church family where I feel like a sister and daughter to many fellow Christians. I find joy, love, peace, and acceptance with them. It really is overwhelming!

THE FRUIT OF A GODLY LIFE

By God's grace, his sons and daughters also live godly lives. Their godliness does not get them into God's family; regeneration does that. But once they are in, they bear a resemblance to their Father and his unique Son, their Brother Jesus Christ.

This fruit overlaps the last one: "This is love for God: to obey his commands" (1 John 5:3). Godliness and love are identifying marks of God's children. "This is how we know who the children of God are and who the children of the devil are: Anyone who does not do what is right is not a child of God; nor is anyone who does not love his brother" (3:10; see also 2:3–4; 3:7–8). In fact, godliness is evidence of regeneration: "If you know that he [Christ] is righteous, you know that everyone who does what is right has been born of him" (2:29).

The power that produces godliness ultimately comes not from Christians, but from Christ. "We know that anyone born of God does not continue to sin; the one who was born of God keeps him safe, and the evil one cannot harm him" (1 John 5:18). Indeed, the Trinity produces godliness in God's children. They are "the children of God" the Father (3:10). "The reason the Son of God appeared was to destroy the devil's work" (v. 8). "No one who is born of God will continue to sin, because God's seed [the Holy Spirit] remains in him" (v. 9).

Does this mean that God's children attain sinless perfection in this life? No. As we saw in 1 John 1:8–10, Christians still sin and frequently need to avail themselves of God's forgiveness and cleansing. Anthony Hoekema says it this way: "Believers, therefore, should see themselves and each other as *genuinely* new, though not yet *totally* new."[2]

Adoption and Regeneration

Adoption and regeneration are two ways of describing how we enter the family of God. Both ideas conceive of God as Father and of believers as his children. In regeneration, he begets his children, giving new life to those who were spiritually dead. In adoption, the Father places adult sons and daughters, former children of the devil, in his family.

Adoption is a legal action, taking place outside of us, whereby God the Father gives us a new status in his family. Regeneration is a renewal of our nature, occurring within us, in which the Father imparts spiritual life to us. Adoption involves a change of legal standing; regeneration is a change of heart. Both are the result of grace and occur in union with the Son of God. As this chapter has demonstrated, regeneration and adoption both give God's children abundant cause to be thankful.

Why does the Bible paint both pictures—adoption and regeneration—to depict our salvation? Because of the awfulness of our plight. We were slaves of sin, in desperate need of being adopted by the Father. Likewise, we were spiritually dead, in dire need of being born again. Adoption and regeneration are two ways in which Scripture magnifies God's grace in stooping to aid us. Each of his children is different, and our loving Father ministers to each according to his or her needs. The example of Pastor Renihan helps us grasp this truth:

> The Lord has blessed my wife and me with five of the most precious daughters. . . . Although they all have similar needs, they are all different; each has her little quirks and points of character.
>
> A need they all have . . . is for nurture and affection from Mom and Dad. At different times and in varying ways, each day finds them in my arms.
>
> The oldest typically will get a hug, usually in the morning. That lets her start her day knowing she is beloved of her father. The next one needs a snuggle and a tickle, and often regular contact throughout the day. I'll walk by her and touch her shoulder or her hair just so she knows that I am thinking about her.
>
> The third and fourth of the sisters usually find my lap at some point in the day. One makes sure my hand is fastened firmly about her, while the other wants me to scratch her back—usually under her shirt so she can feel the scratch of my nails.
>
> The little one gets hugs, kisses, and smiles throughout the day. There is something special

about toddlers. She needs special attention and affection from her parents.

What sounds like a lot of work is really quite automatic. I don't have to go out of my way to give them attention or show them affection. In fact, if I don't find them, they come to find me. . . . When they have bruises or scrapes, I can always elicit a smile and bring comfort. In thunder and storms, they feel safe in my arms. . . .

What a blessed existence for those who are God's people. He is more tender and more loving to me than I could ever be to my children. My love may and will fail at times; His is unfailing.[3]

9

Knowing God,
Our Heavenly Father

I feel so wonderfully blessed every time I think of my family. God promises to bless those who are faithful to him for generation after generation. I have seen this truth worked out in my own family. I can testify, by God's grace alone, that I can never remember a day that I didn't know and love the Lord. This is true adoption!

When I turned sixteen years old (I wasn't allowed to date until then), my father gave me a ring. It has a key engraved on top. On the inside of the band, it has my name engraved on it along with the initials R.W.Y.A. These stand for "Remember Who You Are," and it also has Galatians 2:20 engraved, "I have been crucified with Christ and I no longer live, but Christ lives in me. The life I live in the body, I live by faith in the Son of God, who loved me and gave himself for me." We call it the "key ring" in our family. My two younger brothers both received one when they turned sixteen also. It is our family thing, and we have "key ring dinners" to

we are. I wear it on my wedding fin-
minded that I am a special child of
ng to him, and that I should wait
...ect plan for me in everything, especially
...nate. How wonderful it is that we can be called
children of God! How wonderful to know God as
my Father!

Susan's glowing words encapsulate what this book is all
about. She realizes that she has been greatly blessed by
God. High on her list of blessings are parents who have
raised her to know God as her Father.

Scripture describes the Christian life in many ways. It is
a spiritual battle waged against powerful foes. It is a race to
be run with determination. It is a life of gratitude for grace
received. It is a pilgrimage until we reach our heavenly
home. Viewed from the perspective of adoption, it is a life
lived on earth, knowing God our Father in heaven.

Let's examine three benefits of knowing God as heavenly Father:

> *We address God as Father.*
> *We rely on the Father's provision.*
> *We receive the Father's discipline.*

We Address God as Father

Because of our adoption, we have an intimate relationship with God the Father. Scripture conveys this truth when
it records the way Jesus and believers are entitled to address
God. The time of Jesus' deepest anguish begins in the Garden of Gethsemane. After confiding in Peter, James, and
John, "My soul is overwhelmed with sorrow to the point of

death," he tells them to "keep watch" (Mark 14:34). But three times he finds them sleeping.

Jesus pours out his heart to God: *"Abba,* Father, everything is possible for you. Take this cup from me. Yet not what I will, but what you will" (Mark 14:36). In his hour of distress, when he desperately seeks God's help, he addresses him as *"Abba,* Father." Although the commonly accepted notion is incorrect that *abba* is baby talk meaning "dada," the term is "expressive of an especially close relationship to God."[1] Does *abba* mean "daddy"? No and yes. No, if "daddy" is taken for baby talk equivalent to "dada." Yes, if "daddy" is understood in the way some adult children still refer to a respected and loved father.

It is stunning that, by grace alone, former children of the devil come to know God as Father and receive the right to address him just as Jesus, his beloved Son, did. Scripture expresses this in two ways. First, it says, "Because you are sons, God sent the Spirit of his Son into our hearts, the Spirit who calls out, *'Abba,* Father'" (Gal. 4:6). The Holy Spirit within us addresses God with the same words that Jesus used in the Garden of Gethsemane. Because the Holy Spirit is the Spirit of the Father's Son, he calls out to the Father just as Jesus did—*"Abba,* Father."

Second, the indwelling Spirit not only addresses God as Father for us, but also enables us to do the same. Paul teaches this in Romans 8:15: "For you did not receive a spirit that makes you a slave again to fear, but you received the Spirit of sonship. And by him we cry, *'Abba,* Father.'" Our gracious Father has replaced our bondage to fear with the freedom of his children. As a pledge of our newfound freedom, he has given us "the Spirit of sonship." The Spirit of sonship performs two ministries for us. He assures us inwardly of our adoption (Rom. 8:16). And it is "by him" that "we cry, 'Abba, Father.'" This means that the Holy Spirit, in his role as the Spirit of adoption, enables us to address the God of the universe as Jesus did. This truth has great ramifications.

INTIMACY WITH THE FATHER

Our Spirit-given ability to cry "Abba, Father" points to the intimacy of our relationship with God through adoption. We know the Father so closely that we are permitted to address him as his beloved and unique Son, Jesus Christ, did. That is incredible! How could God communicate the depth of his love for us any more clearly than that? How could he make us feel more at home, more welcome, more a part of his family?

Lawyer David V. Andersen, who specializes in adoption cases, says, "I have begun to see in the lives of adoptive families I work with a picture of God's love—for others and for me." He gives an example:

> In the finalization of a recent stepparent adoption, the judge asked a seven-year-old girl whether she had anything to say about her adoption by her mother's husband. She looked down shyly and then, looking up, said, "Just that I love him." This is what the Spirit enables us to feel toward and to say to God.[2]

As a result of the Spirit's ministry, we enjoy intimacy with the living God, as a young woman named Tennyson relates:

> One aspect of adoption that speaks to me personally is that I am actually a child of God and can address the great God and maker of the universe as my own

Father. This provides me with the intimacy I long for. When I am rejected and unknown by the world, it brings me great comfort to know that they don't know me because they don't know my Father. Someday what I am will be made known. I will be favored because of my Father's name.

CRYING TO THE FATHER FOR HELP

There is a second ramification of our right to address God as Jesus did. Notice that when Jesus cried out, _"Abba,_ Father," he was under great duress. Although I wouldn't limit our crying out to God as Father to times of intense pain, it is appropriate to utter the cry of sonship at such times. Because the Son of God redeemed us, we are in a special relationship with his Father and ours. Consequently, we do not need to be afraid to come to our Father at any time, including times of trouble. He cares for us and wants us to run to him, crying, "Father, Father," when we realize our need for his presence, power, and peace.

Sinclair Ferguson recaps this second point:

> Although he may be broken and bruised, tossed about with fears and doubts, the child of God nevertheless in his need cries out, "Father!" as instinctively as a child who has fallen and been hurt calls out in similar language, "Daddy, help me!" Assurance of sonship is not reserved for the highly sanctified Christian; it is the birthright of even the weakest and most oppressed believer. This is his glory.[3]

We Rely on the Father's Provision

An additional benefit of knowing the Father is that we can rely on his provision. Tracey and her husband rejoice as

117

they begin serving the Lord in Christian ministry. At the same time, they have to adjust their standard of living, since they now make less money than before. Even so, they are willing to sacrifice some of this world's comfort for that of their heavenly Father, who promises to provide for them. Tracey explains,

> At present, our family must live more humbly than we have in the past. It was not my choice, of course—I want to live comfortably—but I am learning to relax in our relationship with God the Father and the inheritance he promised us. I know that we will be taken care of by our Father in heaven. I know that I do not need to rely on my comfort this side of the consummation. I revel in our Father's care now and promise of greater inheritance in the future.

Tracey is learning a valuable lesson: God is our Father, and we can rely on his provision. Jesus emphasizes this in his Sermon on the Mount:

> Therefore I tell you, do not worry about your life, what you will eat or drink; or about your body, what you will wear. Is not life more important than food, and the body more important than clothes? Look at the birds of the air; they do not sow or reap or store away in barns, and yet your heavenly Father feeds them. Are you not much more valuable than they? Who of you by worrying can add a single hour to his life?
> And why do you worry about clothes? See how the lilies of the field grow. They do not labor or

spin. Yet I tell you that not even Solomon in all his splendor was dressed like one of these. If that is how God clothes the grass of the field, which is here today and tomorrow is thrown into the fire, will he not much more clothe you, O you of little faith? So do not worry, saying, "What shall we eat?" or "What shall we drink?" or "What shall we wear?" For the pagans run after all these things, and your heavenly Father knows that you need them. But seek first his kingdom and his righteousness, and all these things will be given to you as well. Therefore do not worry about tomorrow, for tomorrow will worry about itself. Each day has enough trouble of its own. (Matt. 6:25–34)

Crucial for this whole passage is the fact that Jesus twice refers to God as his disciples' "heavenly Father" (vv. 26, 32). The thrust of Jesus' message is that because the heavenly Father takes care of his children, they do not need to be anxious about obtaining the basic necessities of life.

Jesus' reasons why his disciples are to trust their Father and not worry are simple, yet profound. First, he argues from the more important to the less important. Their Father has given them the more important things: life and bodies; they can rely on him to give them the less important things: food to support their life and clothes to cover their bodies (v. 25).

Second, the Son of God reverses his argument and reasons from the less significant to the more significant. Our heavenly Father feeds insignificant birds. Because we are more significant to our Father than birds, he will surely care for us (v. 26). Every time we see a bird fly or hear one sing, it reminds us of our good Father's care for us.

Third, our older Brother warns us that worry is unproductive. "Who of you by worrying can add a single hour to his life?" (v. 27). To the contrary, excessive worry can shorten our life span.

Fourth, Jesus returns to his argument from the less significant to the more significant, this time using flowers as his example. Consider the beautiful lilies of the field. God's children are much more important than flowers. If he so beautifully adorns the lilies, "will he not much more clothe you, O you of little faith?" (v. 30). Jesus' words inspire believers to trust their generous Father to meet their needs.

Fifth, the Son forbids his disciples to live a life characterized by materialism, because that is the way the unsaved live. "For the pagans run after all these things, and your heavenly Father knows that you need them" (v. 32). For God's children to worry excessively about possessions is to live as if they didn't know the Father. For Christians to live materialistic lives is to send signals to a watching world that there is not a Father in heaven.

Instead of worrying, believers are to "seek first his kingdom and his righteousness, and all these things will be given . . . as well" (v. 33). They are not to be preoccupied with material things, but rather with doing their Father's will. He promises to provide for them, and he is true to his Word.

Jesus ends on a humorous note. "Therefore do not worry about tomorrow, for tomorrow will worry about itself. Each day has enough trouble of its own" (v. 34). Our task is to "worry" about doing our Father's will today. Each day has its own troubles, and we'll stumble if we begin worrying about tomorrow's troubles today. Jesus forbids worrying about things that are out of our control. Our heavenly Father controls the future. And we can count on his provision today and tomorrow.

Jennifer knows the neglect of an earthly father and the provision of her heavenly one:

> Abandoned by my biological father at birth, I never had a positive view of fatherhood. How could I? The harshest memory I have of my father was when he refused to give my mom money for medicine I needed for a severe case of bronchitis. My mother, in tears, begged out of fear that I would become more ill or even die. But he remained adamant. I was only about five years old, but that day, I decided that I never wanted to be dependent on a father.
>
> Now, twenty-two years later, through God's grace I have a heavenly Father who was committed to me before I was to him and is committed to me more than I am to myself. He has taught me through his Word to love and forgive my earthly father. He has taught me the love of a father through four godly "fathers," whom he gave me.
>
> He is the One who gives me special gifts and provides for me, his precious little princess. I never saw this so clearly until he led me to step out in faith to the mission field. Growing up very poor and from a rural African-American community, I didn't have many resources for raising missionary support. Yet that is what my Father asked of me, so that is what I did. Wow! I was forever changed by that decision of faith. In my first year as a missionary, not only was I blessed by total strangers with the money I needed

for my salary, but the Lord also provided the finances needed for me to attend seminary.

That was five years ago, and I have not missed a check. The Lord has built my faith through various trials and has taught me that he is committed to providing for me. Even when my support gets low, I know my Father will come through. For five years, I have not known for sure where my financial support would come from in earthly terms, but I have always known where it would come from in heavenly terms. My supporters are only my provision with a little *p*. My Father is my Provision with a big *P*.

I praise my Father that I have not lacked one thing I have needed, including a car, and, most recently, a home of my own. He provided for me a fully furnished Victorian-style home. I know that I didn't deserve any of these things, but my Father in heaven was pleased to give good gifts to me, his precious daughter!

We Receive the Father's Discipline

So far we have considered two benefits of knowing God as our heavenly Father: the right to address him intimately and his providing for our needs. In addition, as sons and daughters of God the Father, we receive his discipline. The most extensive passage on this theme is Hebrews 12:4–11:

> In your struggle against sin, you have not yet resisted to the point of shedding your blood. And you have forgotten that word of encouragement that addresses you as sons: "My son, do not make light of the Lord's discipline, and do not lose heart when he

rebukes you, because the Lord disciplines those he loves, and he punishes everyone he accepts as a son." Endure hardship as discipline; God is treating you as sons. For what son is not disciplined by his father? If you are not disciplined (and everyone undergoes discipline), then you are illegitimate children and not true sons. Moreover, we have all had human fathers who disciplined us and we respected them for it. How much more should we submit to the Father of our spirits and live! Our fathers disciplined us for a little while as they thought best; but God disciplines us for our good, that we may share in his holiness. No discipline seems pleasant at the time, but painful. Later on, however, it produces a harvest of righteousness and peace for those who have been trained by it.

A helpful way to explore the teaching of this passage is to ask, Why does our heavenly Father discipline his children? There are at least three good answers to that question:

> *He disciplines us because he loves us.*
> *He disciplines us to assure us of our adoption.*
> *He disciplines us to produce fruit in our lives.*

HE DISCIPLINES US BECAUSE HE LOVES US

First, our Father disciplines us because he loves us. It is important to clear up a common misunderstanding. Many Bible students incorrectly think that when Hebrews 12 speaks of discipline, it refers to the Father's punishing his children for disobedience. That idea is biblical, but it is not found in this passage. Rather, the discipline spoken of here is the enduring of suffering for God's sake, as verse 7 makes clear: "Endure hardship as discipline; God is treating you as sons." And, according to verse 4, the discipline involves struggling against sin to the point of shedding one's blood, if necessary. The discipline in view, then, is perseverance in difficulties. In light of the historical occasion for Hebrews, we note that the writer includes the section on discipline to motivate his readers to remain true to Christ, even when suffering persecution for their faith.

It is important to realize that the Father brings such suffering into our lives to show his love for us. Mary, who has endured difficult trials in her Christian life, including her former husband's adultery and desertion, loves her heavenly Father's discipline:

> The benefit of adoption that I treasure most is my Father's discipline. "My son, do not make light of the Lord's discipline, and do not lose heart when he rebukes you, because the Lord disciplines those he loves, and he punishes everyone he accepts as a son" (Heb. 12:5–6). I love his fatherly discipline, which assures me that I am his and that he disciplines me because he loves me and is remaking me—giving me that family resemblance.

HE DISCIPLINES US TO ASSURE US OF OUR ADOPTION

Second, as Mary's quotation mentions, our Father disciplines us to assure us of adoption. "The Lord disciplines those he loves, and he punishes everyone he accepts as a son" (Heb. 12:5–6). This is straightforward: because he loves his children, God disciplines every one of them. Although God's children are exempt from the punishment in hell that unbelievers will experience, their Father corrects them in this life. This is one way that he shows them that he is their Father and they are his children. So, when difficult times come our way, we shouldn't question whether our Father is still in control of the world. Instead, we are to remember the words: "Endure hardship as discipline; God is treating you as sons" (Heb. 12:7). The command ("Endure hardship as discipline") is difficult; the explanation ("God is treating you as sons") is sweet. Together they strengthen the assurance of God's children.

The bond between adoption and discipline is so strong that a professed Christian who does not receive discipline from God is a contradiction in terms. "For what son is not disciplined by his father? If you are not disciplined (and everyone undergoes discipline), then you are illegitimate children and not true sons" (v. 8). Experiencing fatherly discipline is a sign of adoption. Conversely, the absence of discipline is a bad sign. It may indicate that the professed Christian is not a child of God at all. Why? Because the Father loves and assures his children, and one way he assures them is by taking them through deep waters.

Kristen contrasts her heavenly Father's gracious, assuring discipline with the mistreatment she suffered at the hands of her earthly father:

> Because I have never known the love of a father, my being adopted by God is a great joy to me. My own father, who passed away when I was young, did things to me that daddies ought not to do to their little girls. . . . How wonderful to experience the true and holy love of God my Father! Now, instead of liv-

125

ing in fear of punishment or abuse, I welcome my Father's discipline because he disciplines me out of love. God is not out to get me; he is out to love me. Although this is hard for me to grasp, my Father continues to assure me of his love. What a joy for a woman who never has done anything deserving that love! What a joy for a woman who as a little girl longed for her father's delight only to be drastically disappointed.

HE DISCIPLINES US TO PRODUCE FRUIT IN OUR LIVES

Third, our Father disciplines us in order to produce fruit in our lives. Verse 10 says it most succinctly: "God disciplines us for our good" (Heb. 12:10). The author argues from common family experience: "Moreover, we have all had human fathers who disciplined us and we respected them for it. How much more should we submit to the Father of our spirits and live!" (v. 9). Many adults look back and respect their human fathers for disciplining them. Think of how important it is for God's children to yield to their heavenly Father's discipline that results in eternal life!

The writer extends the comparison between earthly and heavenly fathers: "Our fathers disciplined us for a little while as they thought best; but God disciplines us for our good, that we may share in his holiness" (v. 10). Here is a contrast between our fathers' and God's purposes in discipline. Our fathers trained us while we were under their authority "as they thought best," that is, as well as they knew how. But our Father in heaven really knows how to do it! He brings difficulties into our lives "for our good," so that we might bear a family resemblance to him in holiness.

Lastly, the author contrasts the pain of discipline with its reward. "No discipline seems pleasant at the time, but painful" (v. 11). This is true in both human and divine spheres. Who has ever enjoyed being disciplined by his or her parents? Nevertheless, most of us as adults look back with appreciation for their efforts. The same is true of our Father's dealings with us. We may suffer now for a time under his discipline. "Later on, however, it produces a harvest of righteousness and peace for those who have been trained by it" (v. 11). Here the writer names specific fruit that comes to those who submit to the Father's training—"righteousness and peace."

Sandra calls attention to this point by describing her family's adventures when taking the children for immunization shots:

> When we take our children to the doctor for immunizations, my husband has the duty of holding them still while the nurse administers the shots. Although it is painful and my children cry, there is no evidence that they doubt or question our love for them. They just want to be held all the more. As God's adopted daughter, my perspective and response should be the same.

God's children will grow if they humble themselves under his almighty hand and look to him in times of trial. They grow in "righteousness," in godly character. In fact, their Father designs the discipline so that they "may share in his holiness" (v. 10). As obedient children, their character is conformed to that of their holy Father in heaven. In addition, they grow in "peace" (v. 11). That is, they learn the valuable lesson of contentment, because they learn to love their Father and find their satisfaction in him in tough times as well as easy ones. That is a valuable lesson indeed.

Conclusion

Every Christian has a Father in heaven. Too often we take this truth for granted. If we allowed the truth of God's fatherhood and our sonship to penetrate our inmost being, we would grow to be more like our heavenly Father. Christian author J. I. Packer powerfully communicates this truth:

> Do I, as a Christian, understand myself? Do I know my own real identity? My own real destiny? I am a child of God. God is my Father; heaven is my home; every day is one day nearer. My Saviour is my brother; every Christian is my brother too. Say it over and over to yourself first thing in the morning, last thing at night, as you wait for the bus, any time when your mind is free, and ask that you may be enabled to live as one who knows it is all utterly and completely true. For this is the Christian's secret of—a happy life?—yes, certainly, but we have something both higher and profounder to say. This is the Christian's secret of a *Christian* life, and of a *God-honouring* life: and these are the aspects of the situation that really matter. May this secret become fully yours, and fully mine.[4]

The Father set his love upon us, the Son redeemed us, and the Holy Spirit enabled us to trust the Son as Redeemer. As a result, we, who by our sinful nature were children of the devil, are now sons and daughters of the living God!

The Father grants many benefits to his children. This chapter has explored three of them: we address him as Father, we are blessed by his providing for our needs, and we partake of his loving discipline.

Matt's words are a good summary:

> To me, the doctrine of adoption is invigorating. It highlights the privilege of intimacy with God my Father. This motivates me to draw near to him. It reminds me that I have a Father in heaven who will meet all of my needs. This moves me to rest in him. It underlines the truth that we can know that we are the true sons of God because God disciplines us in love. This gives me security. For these reasons and more, the truth of adoption makes my heart sing to our Father in heaven, "Hallowed be thy name!"

10

Assurance of Adoption

S ome time ago, a newspaper article said that the residents of Uncertain, Texas were no longer uncertain as to whether or not they lived in Uncertain. This uncertainty was resolved because Judge C. L. Ray had officially decreed that the election resulting in the incorporation of the city of Uncertain, Texas was valid. By a vote of 58 to 11, the city of Uncertain was created. It is northeast of Marshall on Caddo Lake. There is no longer any uncertainty concerning the certainty of the fact that some people live in Uncertain. However, when traveling abroad and filling out forms that specify "place of residence," the residents of this town must write down: Uncertain.[1]

Although, by God's grace, we are not residents of the town of Uncertain, we must admit that too often we are also strangers to the city named Full Assurance of Faith. What does Scripture teach about the certainty of our hope of salvation? How can we grow in our personal assurance of God's grace? This chapter will attempt to answer these questions.

God not only rescues his people from their sins, but also grants them assurance of their final salvation. God assures believers in three ways: by promising in his Word to save them, by giving them the witness of his Spirit within, and by changing their lives. God assures believers of their adoption in the same three ways. The Father gives his children:

The promise of adoption
The Spirit of sonship
A family resemblance

The Promise of Adoption

At times, Christians are confused about the assurance of salvation. Some seek assurance in spiritual experiences. Others scrutinize their hearts in the hope of gaining certainty of eternal life. Still others emphasize their walk with God. However, the most important place to seek assurance is in God's Word. The Father says in his Word that he has adopted us. Paul assures each believer, "So you are no longer a slave, but a son" (Gal. 4:7). We are no longer slaves of sin. Now we are God's children. God declares it in his Word, and it is so.

God the Father's promise of adoption is expressed in two main ways in Scripture. Sometimes the emphasis falls on human responsibility: adoption is by means of faith. "You are all sons of God through faith in Christ Jesus" (Gal. 3:26). Here God states a fact: all who genuinely believe in his Son are sons of God. The same truth is repeated in John 1:12, "Yet to all who received him, to those who believed in his name, he gave the right to become children of God."

Naomi has allowed this truth to sink deep into her soul:

> The personal benefit that I gain from knowing that I
> am adopted by God is a sense of security. I know
> who I am because my identity is found in God the
> Father. Through faith in Christ, I am a member of
> his family. I know that I am loved and can be secure
> in my relationship with him. He is my Father.

At other times, God's Word undergirding the assurance
of adoption is expressed in terms of his sovereignty: adoption is grounded in God's prior choice of his people. "In
love he predestined us to be adopted as his sons through
Jesus Christ, in accordance with his pleasure and will"
(Eph. 1:4–5). God chose us for adoption. This is a wonderful promise of sonship for all who trust Christ as Lord.

Sometimes, however, people nervously ask, "How can
we know that we are predestined for salvation?" Paul answers this question in 1 Thessalonians 1:4–5, "For we know,
brothers loved by God, that he has chosen you, because our
gospel came to you not simply with words, but also with
power, with the Holy Spirit and with deep conviction." We
know that people are chosen by God for salvation by the
fact that they trust Christ. Scripture never instructs us to try
to figure out the eternal counsels of the Almighty. Indeed,
that would be a futile pursuit. Instead, Scripture points us to
the gospel. We know that people are chosen by the fact that
they embrace Christ as offered in the gospel.

God's sovereign grace strengthens our confidence of
sonship. His Word affirms, "In love he predestined us to be
adopted as his sons through Jesus Christ" (Eph. 1:4–5). Ultimately, then, our adoption rests on God's love, pleasure,

and will. It is a great comfort for God's children to rest in their Father's all-powerful arms. No matter what our age, we are all little ones climbing up into the armchair and snuggling contentedly with our heavenly Father.

Whether God's plan or human responsibility is mentioned, the result is the same: in Scripture, God declares that we are his sons and daughters. The bedrock of our assurance is God's Word. Like many of us, Wes struggles with a lack of confidence. His hope builds on God's promises:

> Because I am a son, I have One greater than me, a compassionate and understanding Father, in whom is all my vindication and identity. It is a status that is above my ability to mar or blemish, so it is safe and secure. Yet it is communicated to me so that I *know* it, not kept far away and beyond my experience. In all my mistakes, in all my blunders, in all my low esteem I may receive from friends or adversaries, I can know that I have a Father who scorns me not. If you ask me how I know this, my answer is: When push comes to shove, my assurance that I am a son of God rests on the sure promises of God's Word. It is the Bible's promises of sonship that fortify my faith and my life itself.

The Spirit of Sonship

The primary way that God the Father assures us of sonship is by promising in Scripture to adopt us, but that is not the only way. Along with the promise of salvation, God gives us his Holy Spirit. In the gospel, God gives us a hope of heaven, of future glory. "And hope does not disappoint us, because God has poured out his love into our hearts by the Holy Spirit, whom he has given us" (Rom. 5:5). The Spirit of sonship assures us within our hearts that God loves us. The most important passage of Scripture on this topic is Romans 8:15–16, which says,

> For you did not receive a spirit that makes you a slave again to fear, but you received the Spirit of sonship. And by him we cry, "*Abba*, Father." The Spirit himself testifies with our spirit that we are God's children.

Note that "the Spirit of sonship" sets us free. As we previously learned, this passage teaches that it is the Spirit who enables us to call God "Father" in truth. It is "by him" that "we cry, '*Abba*, Father.'"

There is another ministry of the Spirit mentioned in this passage that is our chief concern at present. The Spirit not only enables us to believe the message of adoption, but also bears witness within our hearts that the message is true. This is what verse 16 means when it says, "The Spirit himself testifies with our spirit that we are God's children." The Spirit whispers in our spiritual ears that we are God's sons and daughters.

Chiefly, God assures us of salvation by telling us in his Word that we are adopted. But he doesn't stop there. He also grants us an internal witness of our adoption. And he assigns a special person to make this witness—God the Holy Spirit. The Spirit of adoption guarantees to us in our hearts "that we are God's children" (Rom. 8:16). This is a wonderful evidence of God's deep love for us. Listen to the comfort that Beth draws from this truth:

I have struggled with bouts of depression since high school, and endured a rather lengthy one this summer and fall. The combination of a change in jobs and the study of how God applies salvation to us became a balm to my spirit. Of all the truths that I have studied recently, adoption is undoubtedly my favorite. I experienced the true witnessing of the Spirit that I am a genuine child and heir of God. For this I praise my faithful heavenly Father.

Beth has drunk deeply from the well of God's grace. The Father has granted her confidence of her adoption by his Word and Spirit. Is it possible to say more about the Spirit's witness with our spirits? My answer is a cautious yes. The Holy Spirit assures us personally, supernaturally, individually, and inscrutably. Each of these adverbs is significant.

The Spirit of adoption assures us personally. Although the matter is debatable, I am of the opinion that this witness is not merely another way of talking about our believing the gospel. To be sure, the Spirit's witness is given only to those who believe the gospel. But it is distinct from our faith in God's Word. It is an additional witness. God bears witness to our sonship both in Scripture and also by his Spirit in our inner being. The Spirit assures all Christians deep within their hearts that God loves them. He intimately fits his witness to their individual personalities, life stories, circumstances, etc., that God is their Father and they are his children.

The Spirit of adoption assures us supernaturally. This is not an assurance that one human being can give to another. It is given by God the Holy Spirit himself. It cannot be obtained by human effort, as if praying or reading the Bible for a certain length of time automatically conveys it. Instead, it is a divine work, as much as creating the world or raising the dead. We can no more bestow the Spirit's witness than we can create life. We are as powerless to produce this witness in our hearts as we are to raise the dead from the grave. We are dependent on almighty God to assure his people within. And the fantastic thing is that he does just that. By his Spirit, the Father assures all of his own that they belong to him.

The Spirit of adoption assures us individually. Each believer in Christ has the inner testimony of God's Spirit. This assurance is not given only to spiritual giants. Pygmies like you and me receive it too! It not only is experienced at times of great spiritual success, but sometimes is felt most keenly at times of spiritual defeat. Just when we groan under our sins, perhaps nearing what seems to us to be our breaking point, then—of all times—we sense the still, small voice of the Spirit within us say, "I love you. You are mine, and I love you."

At such times, we feel so unworthy of the Father's love. The truth is that we are always unworthy of his love; that's what grace is all about. But sometimes it takes our failures for us to realize our desperate need of his Spirit and power. God is a good Father, who loves and disciplines each of his sons and daughters. He made us different from one another, and he deals with us in grace apportioned to our individual needs. One thing we need is assurance, and our Father assures us individually within our hearts that he is ours and we are his.

The Spirit of adoption assures us inscrutably. It is not good for us to pretend to understand more than we do of God's works and ways. Such spiritual pride is out of place for the children of the living God. We are especially ignorant of the works and ways of God the Holy Spirit. Who can explain how the Spirit regenerates those who are spiritually dead (John 3:8)? Who can understand how the Spirit sets apart defiled sinners, constituting them saints (2 Thess. 2:13)? Who can fathom how the Spirit joins lost people to the Son of God, so that henceforth they are united to him (1 Cor. 12:13)? Nevertheless, on the basis of God's Word, we can say with confidence that the Spirit does regenerate and sanctify sinners and join them to Christ. But *how* the Spirit accomplishes these mighty works, we cannot say. We see the results of his working, but cannot predict, control, or fully comprehend it.

The same is true of adoption. We see the effects of the Spirit's work when a slave to sin cries out, *"Abba,* Father"— the first cry of saving faith. But we cannot trace exactly how the Spirit has brought the person to that place. Similarly, we believe in the inner witness of the Spirit because the Bible declares its reality. And we experience it in our own lives. But ultimately, as with all the works of the Spirit, it is inscrutable, beyond our ability to comprehend. In sum, our Father knows better than we, is very gracious to us, and gives us his Spirit to confirm our adoption to us.

Listen to Phil's testimony to the Father's gracious dealings with him by the Spirit of adoption:

> I came to a point of deep pain in 1990, where the outside world saw my spiritual leadership as a campus minister and thought everything was fine, yet there was a lack of authentic presence and power within my personal life. I would look in the mirror at a hypocrite every morning. My wife was very helpful at this time, but my supreme help came from the Lord, as I was asking hard questions about myself, faith, theology, etc. On September 19, 1990, a red-

letter day I'll not forget, I was roaming through Romans, desperate, and came across Romans 8:16. I cannot articulate well what came next, except to say that I experienced that verse. God's Spirit testified that I was his son. And even more remarkably, my spirit joined in and testified that I was God's son. That exchange was so deep that it stands out as my most memorable experience. I don't talk about it much—but it rocked my world, and set me on a course of positive change in theology, direction, marriage relation, and calling. The reality of the Spirit of sonship rocked my world. Perhaps the biggest change was a better alignment between my public life and private life. To God be the glory.

We too glorify God for his working in Phil's life. It is important to add, however, that not everyone shares Phil's experience. In my case, the Spirit's witness in the first year after my conversion to Christ at the age of twenty-one was not dramatic; instead, it was more like a still, small voice. The Spirit's witness does not always conform to one pattern. But the Spirit's witness is always real, whether dramatic or quiet. And that is not all, because the Bible reveals a third way in which God assures his children that they belong to him.

A Family Resemblance

Our dear Father assures us of our adoption primarily by making promises of sonship to us. He promises in his Word that all who believe in Christ are children of God. He goes beyond that and sends the Spirit of sonship on a mission to assure us within that we are God's. The Father assures us in a third way, too: by family resemblance.

I heard a story about a woman who complimented her daughter on her eyes and commented how they looked just like her father's. The daughter replied, "But Mom, I'm adopted!" To that the mother replied, "Oh, yes, I always forget." Like devoted human parents, God loves his children. Unlike human parents, however, he has the power to cause his adopted children to bear a family resemblance. Our Father frees us from bondage and gives us the status of sons (Gal. 4:5, 7). As a result, our character begins to resemble his. The resemblance is far from perfect in this life, but it is real. God begins to bring our lives into conformity with his and thereby encourages us that we belong to his family.

God's children are identifiable. That is the teaching of Romans 8:14: "Those who are led by the Spirit of God are sons of God." Sometimes this verse has been misunderstood. It is not speaking about divine guidance. That is a biblical truth, taught, for example, in Proverbs 3:5–6. But when Paul speaks of being led by the Spirit in Romans 8:14, he is not saying that God guides his children. Rather, the leading spoken of here is akin to the way a sergeant leads a platoon of privates. The sergeant directs and commands the privates; he authoritatively leads them in the way he wants them to go. The Spirit of sonship does the same. He authoritatively leads God's children in paths of righteousness and kindness. He directs them to do the Father's will. And because he does so, they are recognizable. "Those who are led by the Spirit of God are sons of God." That is, the children of God obey the Spirit. They walk in his ways and follow his commandments. This is not how they get into God's family; that is by grace alone, through faith alone in the unique Son of God alone. But once they are in the family, God's children bear a family resemblance to their heavenly Father. Edith, an adoptive mother, knows this from experience:

> People who don't know that my son is adopted re-
> mark how he looks like me or acts like his father.
> This fact helps me to realize that as I grow in Christ
> I will begin to show more and more similarities to
> his character.

This suggests a topic about which the Bible has much to say, but about which many evangelicals know little: suffering. Often Scripture puts privilege and responsibility side by side. That's how it is in this case. Paul speaks of great privilege when he writes, "Now if we are children, then we are heirs—heirs of God and co-heirs with Christ." The apostle adds a qualifier, however, that completes the sentence: ". . . if indeed we share in his sufferings in order that we may also share in his glory" (Rom. 8:17). Those adopted by the Father are his children and heirs! That is a great blessing. Those adopted by the Father share in the sufferings of his Son. That is a great responsibility.

Romans 8:17 has been misunderstood to say that we have to work at suffering in order to qualify for God's family. Of course, that is not true. We are only in the Father's family because of his grace. The key to unlock the verse's meaning lies in the repetition of the word "share": ". . . if indeed we *share* in his sufferings in order that we may also *share* in his glory." Sharing in Christ's sufferings and glory speaks of union with Christ. God has spiritually joined believers to his Son. By virtue of this spiritual union, we are joined to the Son's redemptive deeds—we died with him, were raised with him, etc. This means that sharing in Christ's sufferings is a normal part of the Christian life. It comes with the territory. Belonging to Christ involves sharing in all that is his, including suffering now and glory later.

Consequently, suffering for Christ is one aspect of our family resemblance. Our older Brother, the Lord Jesus Christ, loved us and gave himself for us. His love and self-giving are the very basis of our salvation. When we become a part of God's family, we are united to the Son and share in his sufferings. That's the way it is in the family of God. There is no way into the family except through our big Brother. And once we are in, we are so joined to him that we share in his sufferings.

Some readers may protest, "I don't suffer for Christ. That's for persecuted Christians living in countries like Sudan, Indonesia, and North Korea." I appreciate the honesty of such a protest, but it is misguided. When Paul wrote, "In fact, everyone who wants to live a godly life in Christ Jesus will be persecuted" (2 Tim. 3:12), he wasn't only talking about martyrdom. Persecution takes many forms. Standing up for the Lord Jesus and his interests can be very disadvantageous in American culture today. In school, the workplace, government, the military, and the neighborhood, letting your little light shine can invite insult, penalty, and lawsuit. Of course, we shouldn't seek persecution. But we should be prepared to live for Christ, no matter what the consequences. The prospects of suffering are unpleasant, but seen from another angle, they are incentives to faith, because suffering for Christ is a mark of sonship.

Our Father makes his children's character conform to his own, in part, through suffering, so that they bear a family resemblance and thereby grow in assurance. And sometimes they are a witness to observers. Listen to Hillary's testimony:

My earthly family does not know the Lord, and it has been hopeful to see the steps that God has taken in my life to make me more and more into his likeness and break my sinful patterns. As well, the family resemblance has borne witness to my family members.

Conclusion

God the Father assures us of our sonship in three ways. He promises to make us his sons in his Word, he sends the Spirit of his Son into our hearts, and he changes us so that we bear a family resemblance to him. The witnesses of Word, Spirit, and changed life are manifestations of God's grace working together to strengthen assurance.

Such knowledge should affect us in various ways. Sometimes it pulls us up short, when we forget our identity, as Jennifer explains:

> Studying adoption shows me how often I act like an orphan, and not a daughter of my heavenly Father. I fail to go to him in times of need, thinking I can work it out on my own or fearful that he's going to give me something I don't want or need. In spite of my sin, God's gracious efforts to assure me of sonship are a wonderful reminder to my faith and my heart of God's continuing love for me. His love motivates me to act like the daughter he has made me.

Let us rejoice in our status as God's daughters and sons! And let us enjoy a full measure of assurance by believing his promises of sonship, by listening to his Spirit, and by bearing a resemblance to our dear Father and his beloved Son.

We should praise God for the grace of adoption and the wonderful assurance that it brings, as Amanda explains:

> Learning more about my adoption gives me something that I should have received a long time ago—and yet I have the feeling that I will continue to forget and re-realize it most of my life. We live in a culture where the "search for identity" is not only desperate but fashionable. As I have struggled the past few years to figure out "who I am" and what the Lord wants me to do, I have lost sight of the One to whom I belong. The picture of adoption as familial has made the biggest impact on me. I am very close to my family, but there are times when I think that my relationship to God—his choosing me, my being Christ's sister and coheir in the kingdom—is completely sufficient. My adoption into his family goes so far beyond all of the things I cherish about my earthly family. There is such security in that. My identity is wrapped up 100 percent in Christ's work that made me a daughter of God. I don't have to search for my identity; it is right there and completely sufficient. I rejoice to live day by day, assured that he is my Father and I am his child. I can't imagine anything better than that.

11

The Family of God

*B*eing adopted as a child of God fulfills many of my needs and desires for a better family life and father-daughter relationship. Growing up in a family of nonbelievers, I never heard the gospel. When I became a Christian in high school, I discovered I had a new family. My adopted Christian brothers and sisters were the only true family I knew that was not afraid to express love for one another. God has shown me, as an adopted daughter, the glaring sin in my family of a lack of love. Before being adopted into God's family, I had no desire to have a family of my own in the future, because I assumed it would lead to divorce, pain, and neglect, just as my family growing up did. But he has shown me what his original and real plans for a family are supposed to be. God freely and unconditionally loves his family. This is an example to me, his adopted daughter, of how to love my brothers, sisters, and children in the future.

Whether our experience as children growing up was disappointing like Jennifer's, rewarding, or somewhere in between, her words capture a vital truth—the church is the family of God. By predestinating grace, God the Father is our Father. Because of his work of redemption, the Son of God is our Savior and Brother. As a result, every believer in him is a child of God the Father and a sibling of the unique Son of God. Viewed collectively, therefore, believers are the family of God. Let's explore the implications of this truth for the church, baptism and communion, and church discipline.

The church is the family of God.
Baptism and communion are family ceremonies.
Church discipline is family correction.

The Church Is the Family of God

Scripture presents the church in a number of ways. It is the people of God the Father, the body of Christ, the temple of the Holy Spirit, a part of the new creation, God's flock, Christ's bride, part of God's kingdom, and more. From the vantage point of adoption, what does the church look like? As Paul teaches in Ephesians, the church is the family of God.

Formerly, Paul's readers were not children of God; instead, they were "children of wrath" (Eph. 2:3 NASB). At that time, they were "separate from Christ, excluded from citizenship in Israel and foreigners to the covenants of the promise, without hope and without God in the world" (2:12). But "now in Christ Jesus" they "who once were far away have been brought near through the blood of Christ" (v. 13). What is the result for believing Jews and Gentiles? "Through [Christ] we both have access to the Father by one Spirit" (v. 18). All believers can come to the Father. In addition, all are "fellow citizens with God's people and members of God's household" (vv. 19–20).

It is marvelous: former "children of wrath" are now "members of God's household"! They belong to the family of God. That is why Paul exhorts them, "Be imitators of God, therefore, *as dearly loved children* and live a life of love, just as Christ loved us and gave himself up for us as a fragrant offering and sacrifice to God" (Eph. 5:1). Paul's words describe believers in the twenty-first century as much as those in the first; we are "dearly loved children." The apostle calls upon us to imitate our Father and live a life of love. We bear a family resemblance because we belong to "one God and Father of all" (4:6).

The fact that the church is the family of God should affect the life of the church. Families are to be characterized by unity. So it is with God's family. "There is one body and one Spirit—just as you were called to one hope when you were called—one Lord, one faith, one baptism; one God and Father of all, who is over all and through all and in all" (Eph. 4:4–6).

Futurists agree that America's demographics are changing. George Barna's prediction has come true: "Gone are the days of America as a young, white, middle-class nation. By the year 2000, America will be darker, more wrinkled and from more widely divergent economic backgrounds." Allen Mawhinney has rightly predicted that this points to "a setting in which differences will be magnified and clashes of values will be highly visible. The soil will be conducive to the growth of fear of that which is different and of hatred of that which threatens our style of life."[1]

Events of the past few years justify Mawhinney's concerns. Fear of those who are different has not disappeared from America. But there is another way of life for those who know the Lord, another way of dealing with the effects of the demographic changes that are already coming. Above all people on earth, the sons and daughters of God the Father ought to mirror the unity of his family before a watching world. The church is the united household of God. As the family of God, the church is God's answer to fear and bigotry. Although many churches fall short of the ideal, the unity of the family of God can heal the wounds of believers who find themselves in a different mix than that of their parents.

The family of God should welcome with open arms people of every "tribe and language and people and nation" (Rev. 5:9). One day we will gather around God's throne as a grand choir singing praise to the Lamb who redeemed us with his blood. How good and pleasing it is to our Father if we begin rehearsals now for the eternal song. The church is the family of God, and this should lead us to love and welcome all who come into contact with the church and its ministries. In this way, we can glorify our Father, demonstrate his grace to others, and do something to dissipate the prejudice that too frequently characterizes American life and, sadly, even church life.

The fact that the church is the family of God should affect it in another way: the brotherhood of God's family can heal loneliness. Ours is an age marked by loneliness. The family of God is an important part of God's answer to the isolation of people lost in modern society. The adopted child of God is not an only child; he or she has a unique older Brother, the Lord Jesus Christ. He is magnificent beyond measure, is absolutely faithful, is a close and constant friend, and is able to "sympathize with our weaknesses" and more, to give us "grace to help us in our time of need" (Heb. 4:15–16).

In addition, every child of God has brothers and sisters in Christ. Allen Mawhinney writes, "Every NT writer with the exception of Jude referred to fellow Christians as 'brothers.' It is the Apostle Paul's favorite way of referring to other believers. He uses it 133 times."[2] Paul uses it, not as a stereotype devoid of meaning, but to show deep personal affection. And so does Peter: "Now that you have purified yourselves by obeying the truth so that you have sincere love for your brothers, love one another deeply, from the heart" (1 Peter 1:22).

May God make the church, the family of God, into a haven for those who feel the pain of loneliness. May local churches provide fellowship for those suffering from the effects of divorce. May the Father use his family to provide lonely people with meaningful interaction with other human beings in the service of the King. How blessed are they who discover the satisfaction that comes from investing their lives in ministry to God and fellow human beings, instead of spending more time pursuing pleasure.

Baptism and Communion Are Family Ceremonies

Viewed from the perspective of adoption, the ordinances of the church are the divinely given ceremonies of the family of God. Christian baptism and the Lord's Supper are family practices.

CHRISTIAN BAPTISM

Baptism is the initiation rite that celebrates our entrance into the family. Our older Brother is the prototype. Although Jesus is the eternal Son of God, it was the Father's will that he be baptized. And on that occasion the Father proclaimed, "This is my Son, whom I love; with him I am well pleased" (Matt. 3:17). Of course, Jesus was never a son of the devil, needing to be redeemed. Instead, he was the eternal Son of God who became a human being in order to redeem us.

It is similar for us. At our baptism, the Father in effect proclaims, "This is my dear son (or daughter)." I say this because of Galatians 3:26–27: "You are all sons of God through faith in Christ Jesus, for all of you who were baptized into Christ have clothed yourselves with Christ." This passage teaches that we enter into adoption "through faith in Christ Jesus." Paul connects our adoption with baptism when he says, "For all of you who were baptized into Christ have clothed yourselves with Christ." Being "clothed . . . with Christ" is figurative language for union with Christ. Just as someone puts on a garment to cover his body, so believers are clothed, or covered, with Christ in baptism. They are united as closely to him spiritually as their clothes cling to their bodies physically. Paul here teaches that Christian baptism brings us into spiritual union with the Son of God.

Of course, not every person who is baptized is saved. Millions of men and women have been baptized as Roman Catholics or as Protestants who do not know God in Christ. Even if many invalidate their baptism by unbelief, as many Jews did their circumcision in Old Testament times (see Rom. 2:25, 27), nevertheless God fulfills the promises he made in baptism to everyone who believes. And, according to Galatians 3:26–27, baptism signifies union with Christ, of which adoption is a part. That is the force of the word "for" that connects the two verses: "You are all sons of God through faith in Christ Jesus, *for* all of you who were baptized into Christ have clothed yourselves with Christ." Baptism signifies union with Christ, and adoption is included in that union. Baptism, therefore, is properly viewed as a ceremony indicating adoption into the family of God.

What are the implications of this for church life? Understanding baptism as the initiation rite signifying entrance into the family of God helps to dispel some of the unnecessary mystery attached to the ordinances. There is necessary mystery in baptism and Communion. Explain to me how God uses the preached Word to create life in sinners, and I'll explain to you how he uses the visible words of baptism and the Lord's Supper to unite us to his Son and to nourish that union. But there is also unnecessary mystery attached to the ordinances because of a lack of understanding on the part of God's children. We need simple instruction concerning the meaning of baptism and Communion.

It helps to view baptism as a family ceremony. God the Father makes promises to believers and their children that he will join those baptized to his beloved Son in salvation. When church members promise to help parents in the Christian nurture of their child, they are promising as family members to welcome a new member into the family.

My friend Karsee says it well:

> Fourteen years ago, my parents decided to adopt a baby. I was eleven at the time, and was I excited! A baby brother to play with! Later we got the privilege to go on a TV show called "Wednesday's Child" because my brother had been on that show when he was first born and they wanted to do a follow-up on

his adoption. I don't remember much from the interview, although one thing stands out in my mind, and I doubt if I'll ever forget it. When asked what he did when he first saw his new little boy, my dad said that he looked at the new baby and said, "I am going to love you."

When we are baptized, our heavenly Father announces to all present, "I am going to love you." And the baptized person's fathers and mothers in Christ, along with his brothers and sisters, chime in, "We are going to love you too, because our Father loved us first, and his love overflows from our lives into yours. Welcome to the family, believer in Christ." Or we say, "Welcome to the family, little one. You belong here. We are your new family."

In the past year, my wife, Mary Pat, and I have sometimes struggled to raise our teenage sons for the Lord. We have had much encouragement, but sometimes we have felt like failures as Christian parents. At such difficult times, our source of unfailing comfort and strength to persevere has been the covenant that our Father has made with us and our children. We have rested not in our accomplishments as parents, but in God's sovereign grace promised to each of our sons in baptism. We rejoice, even as we struggle to be covenant keepers, that our ultimate confidence is not in our faithfulness or performance, but in our Father's faithfulness and power. And we are grateful for the prayers, fellowship, and support of the family of God.

THE LORD'S SUPPER

Like baptism, Communion is a ceremony given by the Lord Jesus to the family of God. Seen from the perspective of adoption, the Lord's Supper is a family fellowship meal. This is implied by Paul's words on the institution of the Supper. Because of abuses at the Lord's Table, some in the Corinthian church were "weak and sick, and a number of" them had "fallen asleep," that is, died (1 Cor. 11:30). Paul writes concerning them, "When we are judged by the Lord, we are being disciplined so that we will not be condemned with the world" (v. 32). The Corinthians who suffered at the Lord's hands were experiencing his fatherly discipline of his children. Those who died would not be condemned with the world.

Even when the Father shows his children tough love, he does not condemn them in the way he condemns unbelievers. He treats his family members with love and kindness. Even if they mess up and dishonor their Father, he will not put them out of his family. We risk his temporal judgments and perhaps even physical death, but we are safe in our Father's loving arms.

In 1 Corinthians 11, Paul views the Lord's Supper from the perspective of the family of God. That is, the apostle views God's judgment of believers' abuses at Communion as paternal discipline. This is further borne out by the way he concludes the matter: "So, then, *my brothers*, when you come together to eat, wait for each other" (v. 33). Believers are brothers and sisters in Christ. Their belonging to the family of God is evident at the Lord's Supper.

How should this affect our participation in the Supper? As in the case of baptism, the family perspective can help to dispel false notions of mystery from the Supper. There is mystery, to be sure. We cannot fully explain how Christ, while present at the right hand of God, is also present by the Spirit's power in Communion. Our limitations notwithstanding, Christ is present and offers enabling grace and help to his people. And his people benefit by treating the Lord's Supper as a family meal. The Father is present at this meal, blessing and loving his people. The Father's Son, our Savior and big Brother, is present too. It is he who makes promises to us. He offers us his body and blood in the bread and wine to nourish our faith, to strengthen us, and to invigorate our union with him. We sit with other family members at his Table at this family meal. Together we examine ourselves, confess our sins, and partake of the elements in the meal. As brothers and sisters, we commune with our older Brother, whose Supper this is.

Unlike Roman Catholics in the late Middle Ages who stayed away from the Mass for fear of God's judgment, we as God's children should be eager to come to the Table. It's the family table of the people of God, and by God's grace we belong there. It's not for perfected family members, for they have passed on to their reward and no longer partake of the Supper. They have the fulfillment of the Supper already; they rejoice in the presence of Christ in heaven. We forgiven sinners and adopted members of the Father's family need the Lord's Supper. We come to the fellowship meal of God's family expecting forgiveness, renewal, and encouragement. And our Father and his unique Son give what they promise, even by the presence and working of the Spirit of adoption. May God help us to look forward to the Lord's Supper as much as loved children look forward to coming to the dinner table to be with their parents and siblings.

Church Discipline Is Family Correction

Church discipline, too, is helpfully viewed from the perspective of adoption, as Scripture itself teaches. It is no accident that Jesus uses "family of God" language to instruct his disciples in the importance of exercising discipline in the church. When he teaches that quick reconciliation is God's will, he says, "If you are offering your gift at the altar and there remember that *your brother* has something against you, leave your gift there in front of the altar. First go and be reconciled to *your brother;* then come and offer your gift" (Matt. 5:23–24).

And when Jesus gives instruction for dealing with offenses received, the language is similar: "If *your brother* sins against you, go and show him his fault, just between the two of you. If he listens to you, you have won *your brother* over" (Matt. 18:15). Here we see our Lord using family language to teach his disciples about church discipline. Clearly, discipline is an important practice of the family of God. Church discipline is family discipline. In it, the Father corrects his children through the elders of the church.

Viewing church discipline from the vantage point of adoption can make a big difference in church members' attitudes. Every parent should be able to sympathize with the difficulty of the elders' task in administering discipline in the family of God. We are not to be like cantankerous youngsters who kick and scream when their parents try to correct them. Instead, we are to submit willingly to our Father's discipline, even though it is imperfectly given through the fallible men he has ordained to the office of elder.

Seeing church discipline as family correction also affects those who exercise discipline. As we have learned from the Reformation, there are three marks of the church that enable people to distinguish true churches from false ones: the pure preaching of the Word, the proper administration of the ordinances, and the faithful exercise of church discipline. Unfortunately, the third mark of the church does not shine brightly in some evangelical churches.

Churches that do practice discipline sometimes fall prey to another error—the abuse of discipline. We all have heard stories of sheep who have been bruised by their shepherds' harsh application of discipline. Viewing church discipline as correction within the family of God can serve as a deterrent to abuse. As elders meet together to pray and discuss discipline cases, they must keep in mind that they are leading and correcting professed members of God's family. They are to exercise family correction in the spirit of Galatians 6:1–2: "Brothers, if someone is caught in a sin, you who are spiritual should restore him gently. . . . Carry each other's burdens, and in this way you will fulfill the law of Christ." "Restore him gently" are key words in the job description of elders who represent their own Father and older Brother in correcting their brothers and sisters in Christ.

Conclusion

"How great is the love the Father has lavished on us, that we should be called children of God! And that is what we are!" (1 John 3:1). And our gracious Father has not left us as solitary children. Rather, he has put us into a special family—the family of God. The local expression of this family is your church. Your church is the family of God to which you belong as a member of the family. Learn to love and serve your Father, his Son, and the Spirit of adoption. Grow in your love for, and service to, your brothers and sisters.

Appreciate the church's ordinances anew. Baptism is a family ceremony in which the Father brings new members into the family. The Lord's Supper is a family fellowship meal. Take your place at the meal and receive spiritual nourishment from the hands of the Son of God through his ministers, and your brothers, who serve in his name.

Church discipline takes on new meaning, too, when viewed as family correction. Elders should dispense it with the same gentleness and love they use in their own families, because the church is their family, too. And God's children should not make the elders' job more difficult, but less, by humbly cooperating with them, realizing that their brothers are seeking to exercise family discipline for their good.

May God our Father, the loving Son of God, and the Spirit of sonship teach us to apply the doctrine of adoption to every area of Christian living, both personal and corporate. To the Trinity alone be the glory!

12

Our Future Adoption

arlene shares her personal interest in adoption:

My thoughts on adoption do take on a personal element, because my son is adopted. When I first saw him as an infant, he was alone and without a family of his own, and I remember how my heart jumped when I first saw him at five months old. If my frail human heart could expand like that, I stand in awe of a God who could love me so much to want to include me in his family. I will *always* love my son; he will *always* be my son. He does not always please me, his frailties sometimes cause me grief and concern, but he is mine! What a blessing it is for me to know that I will always be God's child. I am an heir to all that he owns.

We are not all adoptive parents as Darlene is, but every believer will always be God's adopted child and an heir to all that Christ owns. Accordingly, it is time to address our future adoption. Before we see the full flowering of this in the New Testament, let's take a peek at its Old Testament roots. There the adoption of Israel is a present reality. In Hosea 11:1, God declares, "When Israel was a child, I loved him, and out of Egypt I called my son." Because God has redeemed Israel, the nation is already his adopted son.

Old Testament Israel's adoption is also future. In Hosea 1:10, after words of woe, God promises, "In the place where it was said to them, 'You are not my people,' they will be called 'sons of the living God.'" God promises to bring wayward Israelites back to himself as his sons.

The adoption of God's people in the New Testament is also both present and future. Although adoption is mentioned in many passages, there are two where it is the central theme: Galatians 3:26–4:7 and Romans 8:14–25, 29. The former passage deals almost entirely with sonship in the present. The only two future references use the word "heir" (Gal. 3:29; 4:7). By contrast, Romans 8 discloses four future aspects of our sonship:

An eternal inheritance
Redemption of the cosmos
Adoption of our bodies
Conformity to the Son

An Eternal Inheritance

Those who are led by the Spirit of God are sons of God. For you did not receive a spirit that makes you a slave again to fear, but you received the Spirit of sonship. And by him we cry, "*Abba*, Father." The Spirit himself testifies with our spirit that we are God's children. Now if we are children, then we are heirs—heirs of God and co-heirs with Christ, if indeed we share in his sufferings in order that we may also share in his glory. (Rom. 8:14–17)

Thanks to the Spirit of sonship, we are no longer slaves to the fear of God's wrath; we are the Father's children. Because we are his children, we are also his heirs. As heirs of God, we await a glorious inheritance. Just as inquisitive children cannot wait for their father to tell them a delicious secret, so we yearn to ask our Father, "What will our inheritance be like?"

Romans 8:17 is key. When Paul calls believers "heirs of God," he means "not merely that believers are heirs of what God has promised but of God himself."[1] That we are "heirs of God" means that we will inherit God! Remarkably, this is similar to what God already told Abraham in Genesis 15:1: "Do not be afraid. . . . I am . . . your very great reward." And there is more! Romans 8:17 teaches not only that we are heirs of the Father, but also "co-heirs with Christ." We have the same Father as Jesus, we belong to the same family, and, by virtue of our union with the Son of God, his inheritance is ours! Because everything belongs to Christ, his inheritance is the whole world. All believers, therefore, will inherit God and the world (the Trinity and the new heavens and new earth).

Other Scriptures that speak of our inheritance confirm that conclusion. Hebrews 11 takes us from the beginning to the end of God's dealings with his people. Verse 8 records, "By faith Abraham, when called to go to a place he would later receive as his inheritance, obeyed and went, even though he did not know where he was going." After the writer mentions "the promised land," he says, "For he was looking forward to the city with foundations, whose architect and builder is God" (Heb. 11:10).

Where does this point? How are we to conceive of an earthly inheritance of which the Promised Land was an anticipation—a city that God has "prepared" for his people, located in "a heavenly" country (Heb. 11:16)? Our search to learn more about our future inheritance leads us to the end of the Bible. There God combines the earthly and the heavenly when he speaks of "a new heaven and a new earth, . . . the new Jerusalem, coming down out of heaven from God" (Rev. 21:1–2). To be specific:

> Now the dwelling of God is with men, and he will live with them. They will be his people, and God himself will be with them and be their God. He will wipe every tear from their eyes. There will be no more death or mourning or crying or pain, for the old order of things has passed away. (Rev. 21:3–4)

The final inheritance of the Father's children is God himself, living in their midst on the new earth. The promise of verse 7 reassures us, "He who overcomes will inherit all this, and I will be his God and he will be my son" (Rev. 21:7). Romans 8:17, Genesis 15:1, Hebrews 11, and Revelation 21 all point to the same conclusion: we inherit eternal life in the family of God with the Trinity and all of God's children of all ages. We will serve our Father on the new earth and find consummate joy in him, his Son, and the Holy Spirit.

Recently some Christians have shared with me their uneasiness about the Second Coming. They fear giving an account to Christ, embarrassment, loss of rewards, and punishment. For them, Christ's return is a mixed blessing. But in light of our final adoption, we shouldn't have mixed emotions about Christ's return, for then our Redeemer will usher us into the fullness of his inheritance and ours.

The main thing to remember about that day is that it will be a grand revelation of God's grace. God's grace is not limited to the beginning and the middle of the Christian life; it also shines brightly at the end. That is why Peter exhorts us, "Set your hope fully on the grace to be given you when Jesus Christ is revealed" (1 Peter 1:13). When our Savior and older Brother returns for us, he will overwhelm us with his grace. Grace is not only past and present; it is also future. As the Father's beloved children, we will enter into our inheritance and that of our co-heir, Jesus Christ. The new heavens and new earth and God himself will be fully ours on that great day!

A friend named John shares how God has replaced his fear of the Second Coming with joy:

> Often I rejoice in the fact that I have nothing to fear because my heavenly Father loves me so much that he adopted me. Most of all, I have no fear of seeing him face-to-face at the Last Day because he truly is my loving Father, and I am his son.

Is that our testimony too? It can be, if we know the same Father as John.

Redemption of the Cosmos

> I consider that our present sufferings are not worth comparing with the glory that will be revealed in us. The creation waits in eager expectation for the sons of God to be revealed. For the creation was sub-

jected to frustration, not by its own choice, but by the will of the one who subjected it, in hope that the creation itself will be liberated from its bondage to decay and brought into the glorious freedom of the children of God. We know that the whole creation has been groaning as in the pains of childbirth right up to the present time. (Rom. 8:18–22)

Our future adoption has implications for the entire creation. Paul helps believers put their sufferings in eternal perspective: "I consider that our present sufferings are not worth comparing with the glory that will be revealed in us" (Rom. 8:18). Paul's words are reminiscent of 2 Corinthians 4:17, "Our light and momentary troubles are achieving for us an eternal glory that far outweighs them all." Our present struggles, when compared to the glorification that awaits us, fade into insignificance.

Does the apostle tell us more about our future glory? Indeed he does—and in cosmic proportions: "The creation waits in eager expectation for the sons of God to be revealed" (Rom. 8:19). Paul personifies the creation in order to communicate the tragedy of the Fall and the greatness of our restoration. His language expresses a great eagerness of anticipation ("The creation waits in eager expectation . . ."). The creation can't wait for God's sons and daughters to be fully revealed!

Paul portrays the Bible's story as a drama of epic proportions. The first act is set in the Garden of Eden. God is the director, and our first parents are costars. With Adam's fall, the whole creation was plunged into the ruin of the curse. The setting of the drama was marred. "The creation was subjected to frustration"; it failed to achieve the purpose

that its Creator had intended for it. Moreover, God subjected it to "bondage to decay." The curse brought thorn
and thistle, natural disasters, and disease. Consequently, the
apostle likens the creation to a woman groaning in the tra-
vail of childbirth from the Fall until the present.

One glorious truth of Romans 8 is that God will change
the scenery for the last act of the drama of redemption. Before we consider the change of scenery, we need to take a
good look at the star of the last act. He is the last Adam, the
Lord Jesus, who overcomes where the first Adam failed. The
Son of God dies and rises again to redeem his people. As a
result, genuine believers are children and even heirs of God.
As Romans 8:17 declares, "Now if we are children, then we
are heirs . . . if indeed we share in his sufferings in order that
we may also share in his glory." We have been united to him
and receive all his saving benefits, including union with his
death and resurrection.

Because we have been so closely joined to the Son of
God, his revelation at the Second Coming will be our revelation, too.[2] As Romans 8:19 declares, "The creation waits in
eager expectation *for the sons of God to be revealed.*" When Christ
returns, God will manifest our true identity as glorious children. By faith in the Redeemer, we become supporting actors
of him, the star. And—it is amazing to contemplate—the
creation itself will be set free from bondage to decay! The final dimension of our sonship will mean liberation for the creation itself. God will transform the setting for the last act of
the drama of redemption. "The creation itself will be liberated from its bondage to decay and brought into the glorious freedom of the children of God" (Rom. 8:21).

Brothers and sisters in Christ, we have been honored by
our great God and Father! He invests us with great dignity

and glory! Our final adoption has cosmic implications. The ultimate manifestation of our sonship involves nothing less than the redemption of God's cursed creation. The creation gets in on our salvation. Here we learn that adoption into God's family brings great glory and honor.

How this eternal perspective eludes many Christians today! Why do we allow our lives to be dominated by our problems, temptations, and sins? May God teach us to look upward and forward to our final adoption and then to bring that perspective—and all the gratitude for grace that flows from it—to our struggles. That is one purpose of the doctrine of adoption. Listen again to what Romans 8:18 says: "I consider that our present sufferings are not worth comparing with the glory that will be revealed in us." Amazingly, God has even more in store for his children.

Adoption of Our Bodies

> Not only so, but we ourselves, who have the first-fruits of the Spirit, groan inwardly as we wait eagerly for our adoption as sons, the redemption of our bodies. For in this hope we were saved. But hope that is seen is no hope at all. Who hopes for what he already has? But if we hope for what we do not yet have, we wait for it patiently. (Rom. 8:23–25)

Our future sonship involves the adoption of our bodies. We learn of this in Romans 8:23: "We ourselves, who have the firstfruits of the Spirit, groan inwardly as we wait eagerly for our adoption as sons, the redemption of our bodies." This aspect of adoption is future, because "we hope for what we do not yet have" and must "wait for it patiently"

(Rom. 8:25). The "redemption of our bodies" is our resurrection from the dead.

Today many Christians misgauge the shape of the hope of salvation. They correctly understand that for a believer to die is to be absent from the body and present with the Lord (2 Cor. 5:8). But they incorrectly extend this intermediate situation into the eternal one. They imagine that our final salvation will be a disembodied spiritual existence with the Lord in heaven. But that is incorrect. Our disembodied spiritual existence after death is temporary, and, from the perspective of biblical theology, abnormal. God did not create Adam and Eve as disembodied spirits, but as whole beings composed of body and soul together. That is how we live now, and that is how we will live in the eternal state after Christ's return and the resurrection of the dead. So, at present, "we wait eagerly for our adoption as sons, the redemption of our bodies" (Rom. 8:23). The returning Christ will reunite our bodies and souls, and fit us for eternal life, so we can enjoy the Lord and each other forever on the new earth under the new heavens.

Our hope, then, includes awaiting our holistic salvation. This is our *hope*. We should not worry if we are unable to imagine all that this will entail. We cannot perfectly imagine what it will be like, because hope has to do with that which is yet unseen. As Paul explains, "Hope that is seen is no hope at all. Who hopes for what he already has?" (Rom. 8:24). In the meantime, "We live by faith, not sight" (2 Cor. 5:7). As we do, as Paul counsels, let us "wait for it patiently" (Rom. 8:25).

Before Paul speaks of this future bodily adoption, he says, "We ourselves, who have the firstfruits of the Spirit, groan inwardly" (Rom. 8:23). Some readers may be perplexed: what do the Spirit and groaning have to do with our looking forward to the resurrection of the body? When Paul speaks of "the firstfruits of the Spirit," he communicates two important ideas. First, by "firstfruits" he means a pledge in the present that promises fuller blessing in the future. Second, the pledge is the Holy Spirit himself. This implies that believers, all of whom have the Spirit now, will inherit the complete measure of the Spirit on that day.

There are three who groan in Romans 8: the creation (v. 22), believers (v. 23), and even the Holy Spirit (v. 26). At present, our concern is with the second of these. Why do we believers, who have the Spirit of God within us, groan? Precisely *because* we have the Spirit! The Spirit within us longs for the final state of affairs, when evil will be vanquished and God will triumph. Accordingly, we also groan, desiring complete deliverance from our own sins, from those of others, and from a sin-cursed world that begs to be made new by its Creator. Already having the Spirit as a foretaste of the messianic banquet, we crave the full-course meal.

Paul's teaching can help us avoid a false spirituality. In this present life, even with the presence of the Spirit, we groan. At times we all hurt, struggle, fail, are ashamed of ourselves, and are bad examples. If we are honest, we must admit that sometimes we question whether we are even saved.

In a word, *we groan!* We groan for the future glory, for the adoption of our bodies. A time is coming when our present struggles with sin will be a thing of the past. In the meantime, a strong incentive to persevere in fidelity to the Father, even while enduring difficulties, is provided by God's promise of better things in the future. May our hope of resurrection and final adoption strengthen us to live for Christ now.

Perhaps you are bearing a heavy burden right now. That

burden can be the occasion for sharpening your hope of heaven. The day will come when your heavenly Father will give you the biggest and longest hug ever. Anticipation of this hug does not make all your struggles evaporate, but it puts them in a different light. I know some people who *really* believe in heaven. They long to be with the Lord. Every day they think of paradise. Every one of those saints has lost believing loved ones. Their loss has sharpened their heavenly focus. In a similar way, God can use our losses on earth to make us yearn for him and our final deliverance.

Conformity to the Son

> And we know that in all things God works for the good of those who love him, who have been called according to his purpose. For those God foreknew he also predestined to be conformed to the likeness of his Son, that he might be the firstborn among many brothers. And those he predestined, he also called; those he called, he also justified; those he justified, he also glorified. (Rom. 8:28–30)

Our future sonship involves conformity to the Son of God. Paul assures us that God works all things, including sufferings, for our good, because he did for us the greatest good. He brought about our salvation from beginning to end. He foreknew, predestined, called, justified, and glorified his people. The links in the chain of salvation follow one another in succession, almost without interruption: those God foreknew, he predestined, called, justified, and glorified. The one place where Paul elaborates, therefore, denotes emphasis. The apostle highlights a goal of predestination: God "predestined [them] to be conformed to the likeness of his Son, that he might be the firstborn among many brothers" (Rom. 8:29).

In Romans 8:29, Paul returns to the theme of sonship, last mentioned in verse 23. Five features of this passage draw our attention. Four of them pertain to Christ—as the second Adam, the true image, the unique Son, and the firstborn. The fifth feature pertains to us: final adoption involves conformity to Christ.

First, "the likeness of his Son" recalls Adam's creation in the image and likeness of God (Gen. 1:26–27) and his failure as the first man. The term "likeness," when applied to Christ, points to Jesus as the second Adam. This is one of Paul's favorite ways to speak of Christ. He is "the last Adam," "the second man" (1 Cor. 15:45, 47). By his obedience, death, and resurrection, Jesus counters Adam's fall and vanquishes all our foes.

Second, Christ is the true image. The words "the likeness of his Son" point back to Genesis, but also forward to Christ, the true image of God. Adam and Eve were created in the image of God, but Christ is eternally "the image of the invisible God" (Col. 1:15). Our first parents were given dominion and glory, but in the Fall they forfeited these blessings. In Christ, the true image, believers attain a higher standing than that from which Adam and Eve fell. Because Christ "suffered death," he was "crowned with glory and honor," and as a result brings "many sons to glory" (Heb. 2:9–10).

Third, Christ is God's unique Son. Adam was created in God's image to be his son, as is suggested in Luke 3:38.[3] But Adam fell, and he and his offspring became children of the devil. Although God redeemed Israel to be his son

(Hos. 11:1), Israel also failed as the son of God. In mercy, God sent an Israelite, "who as to his human nature was a descendant of David, and who through the Spirit of holiness was declared with power to be the Son of God by his resurrection from the dead: Jesus Christ our Lord" (Rom. 1:3–4). The resurrection broadcast Christ's incarnate sonship. God's children will "be conformed to the likeness of" the unique "Son" of God (Rom. 8:29).

Fourth, Christ is "the firstborn." Colossians 1 presents Christ as the firstborn over both the creation and the new creation. He holds the highest rank over the former because he was God's agent in creation (Col. 1:15–16). He holds the highest rank over the latter because he is "the beginning," the source of the church's life, as "the firstborn from among the dead" (v. 18). Paul's words, "the firstborn among many brothers" (in Rom. 8:29), underscore Christ's preeminence and his sharing of his privileges with his brothers.[4]

Fifth, Paul speaks of final adoption as conformity. He presents Christ as the second Adam, the true image, the unique Son, and the firstborn in order to stress the greatness of the riches that await us. God "predestined" us "to be conformed to the likeness of his Son" (Rom. 8:29). Christ is the goal to which God's people will conform. Earlier in Romans, Paul has already twice described that conformity. By virtue of union with Christ, believers, who already are being conformed to the Son in his death, will also be conformed to him in his resurrection. "If we have been united with him like this in his death, we will certainly also be united with him in his resurrection" (Rom. 6:5). "Now if we are children, then we are heirs—heirs of God and co-heirs with Christ, if indeed we share in his sufferings in order that we may also share in his glory" (Rom. 8:17).

In Romans 8:14–30, Paul wants believers to know that God works all things, even present tribulations, for their ultimate good. Paul teaches us to evaluate present sufferings in the light of future glory. Both come to us through our union with Christ. We should not be surprised when we suffer for him now. And we must maintain a firm hope that as surely as we do so, we will reign with him in future glory. We will be perfectly conformed to the glorious likeness of our older Brother and Redeemer. Hallelujah!

Conclusion

We have seen four aspects of future sonship. We are children and heirs of our Father. We will inherit the new earth and God himself! We are the supporting cast of the Son of God in his drama of redemption. The creation cannot wait to be loosed from the curse and to share our freedom and glory as God's children. In the meantime, we groan while we long for our final adoption, the deliverance of our bodies. Therefore, we eagerly await the day when our Father will raise us from the dead and proclaim to the universe that we are his sons and daughters. We have been redeemed and already are being conformed to Christ's image in holiness. But we are not yet what we will be when our older Brother returns to bring us into perfect conformity to himself. On that day, we will be transformed to correspond to the glory of the true image of God, the resurrected Lord, the unique Son, Jesus Christ.

Notes

Chapter 1: Why Consider Adoption?

1 I acknowledge a debt to Allen Mawhinney, "The Family of God: One Model for the Church of the 90s," *Presbyterion* 19 (fall 1993): 77–96.
2 Sinclair B. Ferguson, *Children of the Living God* (Edinburgh: Banner of Truth, 1989).
3 *Sports Illustrated*, August 16, 1999, 35.

Chapter 2: Is Adoption in the Old Testament?

1 The main ideas for this chapter are drawn from Allen Mawhinney's unpublished syllabus, "The Family of God."
2 John Calvin, *Institutes of the Christian Religion*, ed. John T. McNeill, trans. Ford Lewis Battles, Library of Christian Classics (Philadelphia: Westminster Press, 1960), 2.15.3–4.
3 *Sports Illustrated*, December 20, 1999, 36 (capitals original).

Chapter 3: Slaves of Sin No More!

1 F. F. Bruce, *Commentary on Galatians*, NIGTC (Grand Rapids: Eerdmans, 1982), 203.
2 *St. Louis Post-Dispatch*, January 19, 1999.
3 *St. Louis Post-Dispatch*, December 8, 1998.
4 Charles Wesley, 1738.
5 Josiah Conder, 1836.

Chapter 4: Loved by the Father

1 J. I. Packer, *Knowing God*, 20th anniversary edition (Downers Grove, Ill.: InterVarsity Press, 1993), 83 (italics original).

2 Ibid., 87–88.

3 F. M. Lehman, 1917.

4 Some argue that in the New Testament only Paul teaches adoption. However, I agree with John Murray and Sinclair Ferguson that although John speaks more about regeneration, he also speaks about adoption in these two texts.

Chapter 5: The Son of God, Our Brother

1 *St. Louis Post-Dispatch*, December 9, 1999, A7.

2 John Calvin, *Institutes of the Christian Religion*, ed. John T. McNeill, trans. Ford Lewis Battles, Library of Christian Classics (Philadelphia: Westminster Press, 1960), 3.1.1.

Chapter 6: Redeemed by the Son

1 James H. Moulton and George Milligan, *The Vocabulary of the Greek Testament* (Grand Rapids: Eerdmans, 1930), 383.

2 John Stott, *The Cross of Christ* (Downers Grove, Ill.: InterVarsity Press, 1986), 182.

3 "I'll Never Let Go of Your Hand," by Don Francisco, © 1979 New Spring Publishing, Inc. (ASCAP) (a div. of Brentwood-Benson Music Publishing, Inc.) All rights reserved. Used by permission.

Chapter 7: Drawn by the Spirit of Sonship

1 *St. Louis Post-Dispatch*, November 4, 1998.

2 *World*, June 13, 1998, 45.

Chapter 8: Adopted and Born Again?

1 J. I. Packer, *Knowing God*, 20th anniversary edition (Downers Grove, Ill.: InterVarsity Press, 1993), 201.

2 Anthony A. Hoekema, *Saved by Grace* (Grand Rapids: Eerdmans, 1989), 205 (italics original).

3 Mike Renihan, "Always in the Father's Arms," *Tabletalk*, September 2000, 28–29.

Chapter 9: Knowing God, Our Heavenly Father

1 *The NIV Study Bible* (Grand Rapids: Zondervan, 1985), note on Mark 14:36. See James Barr, "Abba Isn't Daddy," *Journal of Theological Studies* 39 (1988): 28–47.

2 *Christianity Today,* July 19, 1993, 36, 39.

3 Sinclair Ferguson, *The Holy Spirit* (Downers Grove, Ill.: InterVarsity Press, 1996), 184–85.

4 J. I. Packer, *Knowing God,* 20th anniversary edition (Downers Grove, Ill.: InterVarsity Press, 1993), 207–8.

Chapter 10: Assurance of Adoption

1 D. James Kennedy, *The Assurance of Salvation* (Fort Lauderdale, Fla.: Coral Ridge Ministries, 1985), 1.

Chapter 11: The Family of God

1 Allen Mawhinney, "The Family of God: One Model for the Church of the 90s," *Presbyterion* 19 (fall 1993): 79.

2 Ibid.

Chapter 12: Our Future Adoption

1 Thomas R. Schreiner, *Romans,* BECNT (Grand Rapids: Baker, 1998), 427.

2 See also Colossians 3:4, "When Christ, who is your life, appears, then you also will appear with him in glory."

3 See Sinclair Ferguson, *Children of the Living God* (Edinburgh: Banner of Truth, 1989), 6.

4 C. E. B. Cranfield, *The Epistle to the Romans,* ICC (Edinburgh: T. & T. Clark, 1975), 432.

Index of Scripture

Index of Subjects

Robert A. Peterson (M.Div., Biblical Theological Seminary, and Ph.D., Drew University) is professor of systematic theology at Covenant Theological Seminary in St. Louis and a teaching elder in the Presbyterian Church in America.

He is also author of *Getting to Know John's Gospel: A Fresh Look at Its Main Ideas, Hell on Trial: The Case for Eternal Punishment, Two Views of Hell: A Biblical and Theological Dialogue* (with Edward William Fudge), and *Calvin and the Atonement,* as well as numerous journal articles. He is a contributor to *The Evangelical Dictionary of Theology,* second edition, and is editor of *Presbyterion: Covenant Seminary Review.*

A scholar with a pastor's heart, Dr. Peterson has taught extensively in the church since 1973. He and his wife, Mary Pat, have conducted short-term mission trips to Uganda and Peru. They have four sons.